Scepticism and Hope

Scepticism and Hope in Twentieth Century Fantasy Literature

Kath Filmer

Bowling Green State University Popular Press
Bowling Green, Ohio 43403

Annwyl Frank
Ryw'n dy garu di.

Contents

Acknowledgments

If there were any doubt about John Donne's words, "No man is an island," the writing of a book puts paid to it. A writer gathers ideas from many sources—from books, from conversations with colleagues, from odd words dropped at odd moments, from the example of others. But it is not enough to have ideas, even good ideas. The act of writing depends very much on the encouragement one receives from family, friends, colleagues and prospective publishers. In this respect, I am among the most fortunate. I offer my thanks to family and friends, who have had to put up with my mutterings, and to colleagues who have made me think through some of my early ideas.

I owe particular thanks to the Rev. Dr. David Jasper, Principal of St. Chad's College, Durham, who has given me the opportunity of working in the lovely environs of the college, and who has been both friend and mentor. I have a great debt to Professor John Frow, Head of the Department of English at the University of Queensland, who has allowed me to be absent from the Department to carry out research. In particular, I owe many thanks to Ron Marks, Associate Head of the Department and to Dr. Michael Tolley of the University of Adelaide, for their friendship and willingness to read and comment upon this manuscript. And I appreciate warmly my friends in the Mythopoeic Literature Society of Australia, especially my co-founders, Dr. John Strugnell and Dr. David Lake. I owe much to the great fun and fellowship of the Society's conferences, and, of course, to the good friends of the Reverend Hector Fortitude.

My thanks are also extended to others who have helped or encouraged me in particular ways: Stephen Prickett, Regius Professor of English Language and Literature at the University of Glasgow, a foundation member of the Mythopoeic Literature Society; and those students in my 1990 and 1991 Myth, Psychology and Religion course at the School of Continuing Education for their interest and enthusiasm. Warm thanks are due also to David Hughes for some insights into Old Testament Studies, especially with regard to the roles of prophets and priests.

To Professor Peter Jones and his staff, at the Institute for Advanced Studies in the Humanities, University of Edinburgh, Scotland, I owe many thanks for assistance during my Research Fellowship there in the Michaelmas Term of 1990.

I received a Special Projects Grant from the Humanities Group at the University of Queensland to carry out this research, and I gladly acknowledge this assistance. Those students whom I have taught in the Science Fiction and Fantasy courses over the past nine years have also, in a way, inspired this book. They tolerated my ramblings and quite often provoked me into a more critical assessment of my arguments. Most of all, my very warm thanks to my research assistant, Lyn Baer, who deserves much more than this perfunctory tribute. I appreciate very much the work of Margo Higgins and Angela Tuohy, who were responsible for the final draft, and the source of many kindnesses. To my son, Michael Andersen, whose expert attention encouraged my computer to function perfectly, and to my daughter, Rae Kappler, who initiated me into the mysteries of word processing, I am very grateful.

Preface

This book is the result of several years of pursuing the implications of fantasy literature. As it happened (as was *supposed* to happen, as Vonnegut's Bokonon would say), my entry into academic life after working as a registered nurse coincided with the developing interest in this country in structuralist, semiotic and post-structuralist literary theories. My doctoral thesis was concerned very much with elements of hermeneutics and rhetoric in the fictional *oeuvre* of C.S. Lewis, but it became apparent that Lewis was not out of accord, or at least not totally so, with the new theories which I encountered in classroom and common room.

This book is a way of working through the process I then undertook to see if there was any way in which the scepticism of the late twentieth century might itself be subverted, even in what seem to be overtly sceptical works. Is there a deeper structure which is operating in fantasy literature? It will be clear that I think there is.

In Chapter One, I look at the way in which religious discourse has become alien to the secular and sceptical western societies of the twentieth century. There is real discomfort when religious discourse appears either in the popular press or in literary representations. Believers become marginalised in society. (I should point out that I write from a Christian perspective, since that is my background; but I believe that the main points in this book would hold true for those from other religious traditions.) But even in a secular society, there is still a psychological need (one might even use the stronger word *will*), if not to believe, then at least to hope. And, as I hope to show in the chapters which follow, this need is met in the literature of fantasy.

Twentieth century fantasy has emerged from a long tradition of religion and philosophy, and it has adapted itself to provide gods and heroes whom readers might worship and in whom they might transcend themselves. I do not argue that the literature of fantasy is "about" religion; rather my argument is that fantasy *speaks* religion, that it operates in the same space and uses the same devices as the discourse of religion, and does so largely to the same end: the articulation of hope.

In Chapter Two, I discuss the role of author as priest, the person from whom religious utterances are issued. Again, I look at the traditions of last century in order to show that this has been almost an inevitable appropriation, given the rapid development during the last century of sceptical philosophies and evolutionary science.

The succeeding chapters deal with works of fantasy which have been enduringly popular this century, beginning with the epic trilogy which revolutionized public perceptions of the genre, J.R.R. Tolkien's *The Lord of the Rings*. Other authors from whose works I have selected examples for discussion are C.S. Lewis, Peter Beagle, Susan Cooper, Madeleine L'Engle, George Orwell, Russell Hoban, James Thurber, Kurt Vonnegut, Jr., Alan Garner, Ursula Le Guin and Patricia Wrightson.

Chapter Twelve surveys the historical emergence of Fantasy from Romanticism and examines the way in which it continues the Romantic tradition, elevating the role of the Imagination to a quasi-Divine faculty, and the role of the author to that of prophet and priest. It reaffirms that, in the present sceptical age, Fantasy offers its readers a vision of the marvellous and the wonderful, and through that vision, the clear articulation of hope for humanity.

I should, perhaps, point out that my selection of works for discussion has been entirely subjective—as most selections of this kind inevitably are. I have chosen authors and works with which I have become most closely familiar, and which, through teaching, research and personal experience, I have come either to value or to recognize that others find valuable. The works chosen for Chapter Eleven are those which I have reviewed in the last eighteen months, and which have had at least an initial popularity. I am, of course, aware that twentieth century fantasy is a vast field, which even David Pringle's "Hundred Best" barely taps.[1]

So this cannot be the last word in research of this kind. I hope it is only one of the first, and that if I achieve nothing more, others will begin to think about these issues and offer their insights into what is undoubtedly a compelling and provocative field of study.

Chapter One
Fantasy and the Displacement of Religious Discourse

And all should cry, Beware! Beware!
His flashing eyes, his floating hair!
Weave a circle round him thrice
And close your eyes with holy dread,
For he on honey-dew hath fed,
And drunk the milk of Paradise.
Coleridge, *Kubla Khan*

In an essay titled "Poetry and Prayer," American critic Nathan A. Scott, Jr. writes:

. . . a radically secular literature may have a profoundly fruitful religious function to perform. For, by the very resoluteness with which it may plunge us into the Dark, it may precipitate us out of our forgetfulness, so that, in a way, our deprivation of the Transcendent may itself bring us into proximity to its Mystery. (208)

In the same collection of essays is a piece by J. Hillis Miller, who believes (or believed when he wrote the essay) that twentieth century literature could transcend nihilism, the absence of the withdrawing God, by presenting a divine and immanent presence. He observes:

If any spiritual power can exist for the new poetry it must be an immanent presence. There can be for many writers no return to the traditional conception of God as the highest existence, creator of all other existences, transcending his creation as well as dwelling within it. If there is to be a God in the new world it must be a presence within things and not beyond them. The new poets have at the farthest limit of their experience caught a glimpse of a fugitive presence, something shared by all things in the fact that they are. This presence flows everywhere, like the light which makes things visible, and yet can never be seen as a thing in itself. It is the presence of things present. . . . (186)

It is perhaps interesting to note that of these two critics, it is Hillis Miller whose attitude to spirituality in literature corresponds most closely to the attitudes and ideas developed by George MacDonald, the author who has had the most profound influence on two of the seminal fantasy writers of this century, C.S. Lewis and J.R.R. Tolkien. In MacDonald's adult fantasy novel, *Lilith*, the spiritually regenerated Mr. Vane exclaims:

1

2   Scepticism and Hope

> I lived in everything, everything entered and lived in me. To be aware of a thing, was to know its life at once and mine, to know whence we came, and where we were at home—was to know that we are all what we are, because Another is what he is! (243)

In other words, there is some evidence to suggest that there has been a shift of literary theological approaches from the notion of the Transcendent God to that of the Immanent God, the fulfilment of the Gospel words, perhaps, that "the kingdom of God is within you." That such views have a particular relevance to the literature of Fantasy can be seen by watching fantasy at work, as it were, constructing realms from the imagination. There is certainly a sense in which worlds— including the mundane world—have existence only in the perception and imagination of the individual, and that issues of religious faith and hope also are individual. In a secular world, indeed a world in which scepticism and nihilism have more currency and are regarded as more valid than religious belief, the discourse of religion becomes increasingly alienated from the concerns of those who are most closely bound to the mundane preoccupations of, say, earning a living or simply managing to survive in the face of government intervention in living standards. Nevertheless, I want to argue that there remains a basic hunger for religious belief, and for that most enduring of the human emotions, the hope that things will, in some way, get better. Hope, after all, is what sustains most human beings in the face of dire adversity; when hope is lost there is no further will to live, indeed there seems to be no point at all to life.

It seems to me that fantasy literature does two things: it comes to terms with the existential *angst* of the twentieth century, and accepts the reality of the scepticism that pervades the external world. Indeed the same kinds of scepticism to be found in post-modern critical theories can be seen in open-ended narratives, the refusal of closure, self-reflexivity and the proliferation of pessimistic projections for the future which are characteristic of twentieth century fantasy. Nevertheless, I believe that fantasy is sceptical only superficially; if one looks more deeply at the texts of fantasy, one finds unmistakably the articulation of hope. It is this latter, deeper reading of fantasy texts with which I want to deal in this book, showing how the issues of faith and doubt, the particular fears and apprehensions of the late twentieth century, are encompassed in the range of imaginative writing, and how fantasy writers, regardless of their particular *Weltanschauung* or for that matter their *Weltschmerz*, nevertheless find within the generic constraints of fantasy the ability to articulate, and the possibility of arousing, hope.

The twentieth century has been the age of "future shock," the age which has been most sorely buffeted by global war, the age in which whatever certainties surviving from an earlier age have attracted the most profound doubts. A partial response to this in the last quarter of this century has been the resurgence of a great number of simplistic religious sects, all offering some form of deliverance from the existential *angst* which has so characterized these latter years. Invariably, however, their mix of mysticism, New Age self-actualisation and sheer exploitation has led many only to further disillusionment and disbelief. This is a secular age, an age in which the discourse of religion has been suppressed and in which belief has become the hallmark of the minor zealot, the crank in the marketplace with glazed eyes and a handful of cheaply printed tracts.

There is also, among those who have retained the practice and form of a traditional religion, a certain discomfiture aroused by confrontations with discourses from opposing camps. Traditional or "Mainline" Christians are often offended by the "Repent, be saved, be washed in the Blood of the Lamb" emotional discourse of the Fundamentalists, who in turn are dismayed by what they see as wishy-washy underminings of God's Laws by world-serving liberals. Christianity is divided by different discourses; but the divide between Christianity and other world religions is similarly established through language. For example, the outrage at British author Salman Rushdie's novel *The Satanic Verses* has been primarily linguistic in its expression—oral interviews, slogans and banners at rallies, newspaper items and the like. So far, Rushdie, albeit in hiding, has not been murdered. But the discourse of Islam has been condemned by smug Christian groups whose acquaintance with the history of the Christian church is selective to say the least. Religious discourse, including that of the Christian Church, has long been perceived to be judgmental, authoritarian and, in some instances, simply cruel. One recalls the impassioned response of a British woman after the long awaited Papal Encyclical, *De Humanae Vitae*, which was released in the 1960s: "How many Catholic bishops have died in childbirth?"

It is difficult to mount a defense of religion in the face of the accumulation of damning evidence against it, but when belief is excised from the human experience, its absence is painful. The Swiss psychiatrist Viktor Frankl observed in the concentration camps of Nazi Germany a phenomenon of survival which prompted him to develop his "logotherapeutic" psychology. Of those who were not taken to gas chambers, survival was more probable, Frankl noted, in those who had some *reason* to survive. This reason might be religious faith; but it might be as simple as the desire to return to a beloved house, or to see to the welfare of a pet animal. Survival, Frankl noted, depended on some kind of *hope*. He writes:

Man's search for meaning is a primary force in his life and not a 'secondary rationalisation' of instinctual drives. This meaning is unique and specific in that it must and can be fulfilled by him alone; only then does it achieve a significance which will satisfy his own *will* to meaning...

4   Scepticism and Hope

A poll of public opinion was conducted a few years ago in France. The results showed that 98 per cent of the people polled admitted that man needs "something" for the sake of which to live.... (99)

An Australian disciple of Frankl, psychiatrist Julian Bulnois, believes that humans move towards psychological wholeness when they can leave behind the stages of dependence and autonomy and progress to the stage of reaching out to others, seeing themselves as part of a network of human relationships.[1] There are variations on this theme; for example, Thomas Harris, in his *I'm Okay, You're Okay* and subsequent books, encourages his readers to aim for adult-adult transactions in daily encounters. These transactions are based on the formula which is the title of his book: "I'm okay, you're okay." And to be "okay," in his terms, means to achieve self-acceptance and the acceptance of others, and it requires a mature acceptance of identity, not only of oneself but also of one's fellows.

The *angst* of this secular, nihilistic age is explored in the growing number of science fiction and fantasy texts which address, as worthwhile fantasy has always done, human concerns, psychological and spiritual. Within the constraints of these genres there is now a discourse which addresses itself to these concerns in a manner which suggests that religious discourse has been displaced from its contextual siting in the social rituals of worship to the private experience of engagement with a written text. I do not mean to propose that the authors of science fiction and fantasy texts are "putting religion into the story," as it were, although it is clear that some authors do so. Rather I believe that the discourse of the fantastic is itself a form of religious discourse, with all the features of didacticism, persuasion and emotive language which have traditionally been associated with the discourse of religion.

A look at some titles confirms this: *The Dark is Rising, Till We Have Faces, The Word for World is Forest,* and so on. Other titles are more enigmatic, but their content nevertheless reveals the same engagement with essentially religious issues of scepticism, belief and hope.

The "religious" discourse of science fiction and fantasy is, not surprisingly, as varied as the range of religions to which its authors have access. And yet one can discern on closer analysis that there is a commonality of theme which links works in these genres, despite their diverse approaches. It is the tension between scepticism and belief, the dialectic which is lived out in every human life, the ultimate requirement which each individual faces to make some kind of choice.

The discourse of fantasy is presented in the same forms as those used in religious scriptures—metaphor, myth and symbol. These devices appeal to reason, imagination and emotion, and allow for the same kinds of experience in reading as do religious texts. Moreover, fantasy and science fiction are no less didactic than sacred texts. And indeed if they engage with the issues of doubt and disbelief, they do no more than the sceptical book of Ecclesiastes in the Bible, the great number of doubting and/or sulking prophets, or the frankly disbelieving apostle Thomas of the New Testament.

In this book, then, I want to argue that the literature of fantasy and science fiction has a significant part to play in the religious concerns of the late twentieth century, and that the discourse of religion, marginalized not only by a consumerist and materialist society, but also by the anti-theological discourse of certain contemporary literary theories, is legitimized in these genres.[2] It is said that energy never dissipates, but merely changes its form; so the linguistic expression of the most profound human needs is displaced from religion to literature, but to a certain *kind* of literature which makes available the symbolic forms by which ontological and metaphysical concerns might be addressed. This displacement is, of course, nothing new; the very encoding of religious revelations and doctrines into scriptures which form the core of any culture's literature has ensured that there is a symbiotic relationship between literature and religion. And of course the twentieth century owes to Matthew Arnold the notion that literature constitutes a secular religion; although what I will argue in the pages that follow is that in fantasy literature the notion of secularity itself is displaced in favor of affirmative metaphysics.

The displacement of religious discourse has been accelerated in the sceptical milieu of this century. There is, surely, more than a coincidental relationship between this process and the development of sceptical theories which have been applied to the writing and reading of texts in the last few decades. The sceptical impetus of postmodernism, however, seems almost to have run its course; many critics are finding the French philosophies at the heart of the most recent developments in sceptical and in some cases nihilistic theory to be untenable. There is nevertheless some value in the questions posed by these theorists; after all it should be clear that theorists are merely asking questions about the world, not dogmatically affirming that they have answers. Often the concerns they address are not far from those with which fantasy and science fiction take issue.

Of course, it is a mistake to attribute only to the twentieth century the development of sceptical thought, whether is is manifested as scepticism over various aspects of religious belief, or more generally, over the nature of language and meaning. Its history spans the centuries, although it is true that scepticism is more characteristic of some ages than of others. But I think it is valid to say that the scepticism which pervades twentieth century thought has developed out of the sceptical attitudes which had both literary and philosophical currency in the last century. The Romantics, both German and English, had particular questions to ask about the nature of the universe and the place of the poet within it; and today's science fiction and fantasy owe a great deal to the Romantic tradition. I apply the term "scepticism" to doubts and questions not only about the nature and function of religion, but also about the way language expresses meaning, which in Christian theology at least is closely related to religious belief, since Christ is seen to be the Incarnation of the Divine Logos: "In the beginning was the Word, and the Word was with God, and the Word was God" (John 1:1).

Samuel Taylor Coleridge is often taken to be the greatest English literary theorist.[3] Coleridge is a pivotal figure because in him converge a number of influences, especially that of German Romantics such as Schelling and Friedrich Schlegel. The common theme in German Romantic thought is the notion, not of some consolatory absolutism, but of growth, change and becoming. From Coleridge comes, of course, the seminal definition of the Imagination, the human faculty which is the *sine qua non* not only of writing, but also of reading, literature; although I shall focus, for the present purpose, upon fantasy literature. It is found in his *Biographia Literaria,* Chapter XIII:

The IMAGINATION then, I consider either as primary, or secondary. The primary IMAGINATION I hold to be the living Power and prime Agent of all human Perception, and as a repetition in the finite mind of the eternal act of creation in the infinite I AM.

The secondary Imagination I consider as an echo of the former, co-existing with the conscious will, yet still as identical with the primary in the *kind* of its agency, and differing only in *degree*, and in the *mode* of its operation. It dissolves, diffuses, dissipates, in order to recreate; or where this process is rendered impossible, yet still at all events it struggles to ikdealize and to unify. It is essentially *vital*, even as all objects (*as* objects) are essentially fixed and dead. (Coleridge 202)

Here, of course, Coleridge refers to the primary human imagination and the creative power of perception, in which he describes the process of perception as an imitation of the divine *fiat,* by which all things were created *ex nihilo.* By perception, the elements of the created world are created anew, gaining a reality in our minds which, unperceived, they could not possess. This appears to be very strong language, imputing to the human mind the quality of divine creativity. When Coleridge defines the Secondary Imagination, he reinforces the notion of human creativity, since the secondary element of the Imagination is the re-creating faculty which impels the expression of things perceived, through (for example) artistic forms—in Coleridge's instance, poetry, but also in art and music. The Secondary Imagination recombines perceptions to present them with new insight, embodying them in new modes of expression. Underlying this mode of the Secondary Imagination is the desire to create unity from growth—a concept which Coleridge derived from the German philosopher Friedrich Schlegel. This notion of growth and creativity through becoming and through change has been neatly expressed, as David Jasper has pointed out, by Victor Hugo in his 1826 Preface to *Odes et Ballades*, where he criticizes the tendency to systematize contemporary French architecture:

> A gothic cathedral presents a wonderful order in its naive irregularity; our modern French buildings, to which Greek and Roman architecture has been so clumsily applied, offer merely a regular disorder. Anyone will always be able to make a regular work; it is only great spirits who know how to order a composition. The creator, with elevated vision, shapes; the imitator, who observed from close up, systematizes. (Hugo 1:265, cit. Jasper 17)

Hugo here expounds the virtue of "irregularity" against strict form and structure in much the same way as the sceptic will argue for chaos and incalculability against divine providence and order. Coleridge too draws from German Romanticism the notion of restless progress, a quest in some sense for a lost wholeness. The impetus behind Coleridge's thinking is not so very different from that which lies behind sceptical critical theories, especially those which have been collectively called "Deconstructionist." Many Deconstructionist theorists seem to offer a negative metaphysics, an anti-theology, an attack *contra fidem et ecclesiam*, to which others, with a more traditional background of religious belief, take exception. But if Coleridge emphasizes the notion of re-creating, he does so after "deconstructing" in the process of dissolving, diffusing, and dissipating.

The effect of these theories and the influence of Romanticism on the literature of fantasy is fundamental to this study, since I think it can be shown that while fantasy also "deconstructs" and undermines certain assumptions about the world, it also sets in place a new iconography of the sacred which in turn subverts the sceptical imperative which many believe lies at the heart of fantasy literature.

Deconstruction has been formulated in many ways, but essentially it is understood to be an operation which undermines and subverts, demystifies and destabilizes what have been considered "traditional" certainties and authorities, along with notions of privileged readings, illusions of objectivity, or the possibility of interpreting a text. In other words, Deconstructors categorically assert that all texts (and spoken language, since that too is seen as a kind of text), is subject to deconstructing, and that all language covertly undermines what it asserts. The fundamental premise is that there is a privileged or preferred reading to language and that this reading must be undermined, subverted, denounced, opposed, stood on its head—so that ultimately there is no preferred reading. However, in order to achieve that state of non-reference, Deconstructionists have to retain what they perceive as traditional reference in order to annihilate it. In other words, if there *were* no referential meaning or traditional view, there could be no Deconstruction (Ellis 261).

But if the term "Deconstruction" is new, nothing else about the philosophy and the approach is original. After all, this is simply a restatement of what Christianity has done with the traditional Jewish texts of the Old Testament. This is an issue addressed by Susan Handelman in her incisive work *The Slayers of Moses*. Handelman clearly shows how Christianity subverted the Old Testament texts so that their preferred readings were undermined, especially those with specific Messianic references. After Christ, Christianity subverted even more the notion of the Word, adopting the Greek concept of the Logos as Sign rather than the Hebrew concept of the Word as entity (163-178). More pertinently, Christ Himself, in the Sermon on the Mount, deconstructed, as it were, the basic tenets of the Jewish law.

One other fact that sceptical philosophers choose to ignore is that adherents of any belief constantly engage in an internal dialectic between belief and doubt. Believers are not sure, or at least they are not always sure; even in the most fervent fundamentalist meetings there will be some who ask for prayer to take away their doubts. Coleridge suggests that when a reader engages with a text, there is a "willing suspension of disbelief." J.R.R. Tolkien takes issue with this, however, and asserts that rather there is what might be termed "an agreement to believe" in a secondary, author-created world. When one is conscious of "suspending disbelief," Tolkien claims, that fantastic text is not successful (36-37). Now this point might be extrapolated in regard to the experience of engaging with contemporary theoretical texts, during which a reader must consciously and often quite violently "suspend belief." Indeed, this is what *must* happen, for as Deconstructionist critic Christopher Norris points out, to try to apply Deconstructionist theories to the practice of mundane existence is impossible, since "that way madness lies" (Norris 5). What fantasy literature does, then, is to instigate a process by which "suspended" belief can be accommodated, and if belief is not fully recoverable from the experience of reading, then at least it can be compensated for by the articulation of hope.

It has been said that when Coleridge tries to rely on a rigid prescriptive framework for spiritual apprehension, he does not succeed. But he *does* succeed when he recognizes the inadequacy of that framework, as when he writes, "Christianity is not a Theory, or a Speculation, but a Life. Not a *Philosophy* of Life, but a Life and a Living Process..." (Prickett 183n).

With this acknowledgment comes the recognition that Life is not a rigid, systematized "preferred reading" in any sense but rather a state of change, development and growth—a state in which certainties and absolutes belong to the careless egotism of youth. Wisdom is, simply, the acknowledgement that we don't and can't know all things absolutely, but that we can learn from our experiences those aspects of truth which pertain to us. By the same token, we cannot negate the validity of experiential truth for someone else. Reading is not merely interpretation or decoding, it is imaginative experience. But the very role of the imagination is one of constant subversion and undermining, a destabilizing, as it were, of dogmatic assertations in literature and in theory; and I think Coleridge's definition of the Imagination allows for this destabilizing process.

For even when Coleridge affirms the divine element in human perception and creativity, he builds in his own subversive, proto-deconstructive device. Words such as "repetition," "finite," "echo," "dissolves," "diffuses," "dissipates," "rendered impossible" and "struggles" seriously undermine any notion of absolutism. It is apparent that Coleridge seeks to affirm something while admitting the perplexities of his affirmation, since even the persuasive concept of recombining created elements is expressed through the negative words "dissolve," "dissipate" and "diffuse," when Coleridge could have said simply, "It recombines." But clearly to dissolve, diffuse or dissipate is to *weaken* something, not merely to "recombine" it with other elements. At the heart of what has been taken to be a grand affirmation of faith in human creativity is subversion by the very language used to express it. It affirms, doubts and denies in a clear example of "proto-deconstructive prose"; it questions, and as it does so, it strives and searches for truth, since truth, or what truth there is to which humanity has access, is achieved primarily by asking questions. Coleridge, however, is far from Deconstruction as it is currently known and practised, since what he constantly aims for is creativity, growth and meaning.

In fantasy literature, characters strive and search for some often unattainable goal, or a goal which, when reached, falls short of expectations. But although fantasy does not always fulfill readerly expectations, it nevertheless does not leave them with nothing. Fantasy commonly offers some kind of closure, even if that closure is implied, although open endings also leave room if not for a certain kind of faith, then for a certain kind of hope. Through symbol and metaphor, fantasy also creates and quests for meaning.

One might turn for an example of hope in operation to the twentieth century's most influential fantasy text, Tolkien's *The Lord of the Rings*. It is generally assumed among Tolkienist critics that this epic work fulfills the criteria set out in Tolkien's theoretical essay, "On Fairy Stories," in providing escape from the "prison" of the mundane world, the "recovery" of a sense of enchantment in perceiving mundane reality, and "consolation" in the promise of redemption and eternal life (Tolkien 50-60). It is with this last that I think we can take issue.

The Lord of the Rings is a book preoccupied with the power of evil. Even the title refers, not positively to the triumph of good, but negatively, to the evil entity who embodies power-lust, greed, domination and blind rage. The verse which appears as the book's epigraph is also concerned with doom, devilry and destruction. Before the narrative actually commences, the book develops a heavy mood of pessimism. It might be argued that there is a marked shift at the conclusion to the notions of restoration and optimism, but such an argument is based upon a fundamental misunderstanding of the book's underlying theology. In my view, as I explain in Chapter 3, the pessimism never lifts. But we are speaking here of a surface decoding; at the deeper level there is certainly a recapitulation of hope and belief.

Something of the same kind of double-layering of theme occurs in other fantasy works, such as Russell Hoban's adult novel *Riddley Walker* and his children's book *The Mouse and His Child*, the work of Alan Garner, Madeleine L'Engle, Susan Cooper and Peter Beagle, and even the painfully pessimistic *Nineteen Eighty-Four* by George Orwell. In this last novel, readers need no qualifications for or pretensions to the roles of critic and theorist to acknowledge that here is a most damning tirade against the futility of hope. But even when there seems to be no possible decoding which could subvert the pessimism which pervades this text, there is still accessible at the deeper levels of signification the notion that the novel has been written to defend certain values and beliefs rather than to celebrate their extinction. In other words, as I hope to show in a later chapter, Orwell too offers his readers a quantum of solace in the articulation of hope.

And it is in the articulation of hope that fantasy literature has displaced religious discourse in the twentieth century. It is often overlooked that Hope is one of the cardinal virtues. In Christian theology hope is seen to be intrinsically bound up with the operation of faith and love, but it is, I think, the basis for both. Hope has been somewhat devalued as a rather damp and insignificant emotion, but in fact it is as psychologists know well, a sustaining force in human experience. When religious discourse fails to offer hope on a personal as well as on the cosmic scale, it no longer speaks to the vast majority of human beings who refuse dogmatic statements and platitudes. Fantasy provides hope that heroes will arise and take up the cause of a battered twentieth century humanity. They deliver what politicians offer but cannot provide, the hope that somehow some sense will come of it all, that there is a purpose, and that things might get better. Without hope, human experience and existence could not continue; loss of hope means loss of the will to live. It is in the context of this issue of hope in the midst of scepticism, hope in the face of nihilism, hope in the face of disillusionment, that the displacement of religious discourse has been achieved. And fantasy literature, seen in this light, takes on a profound significance not only in relation to critical theories, but also in relation to human spirituality and to the enrichment of human life in the mundane world.

Chapter Two
The Author as Prophet/Priest

Prophets...[they] to them will speak
A lasting inspiration, sanctified
By reason, blest by faith: what [they] have loved
Others will love, and [they] will teach them how.
Wordsworth, The Prelude, xiv: 444-47

The traditional utterances of religious discourse are made by a person empowered to do so by ritual ordination of some kind or another. While in the Old Testament, the roles of priest and prophet were distinct,[1] the practice in orthodox Christianity has been to combine them. Society looks to its priests and prelates for the prophetic word in times of national or global crisis, and it is in this sense that I use the terms. In the historical "mainline" Christian churches, this role is filled by the priest or minister. Even in the climate of change which pervades the late twentieth century church, the formal discourse of religion remains very much the primary province of the prophet/priest who presides at the services of worship, who delivers the sermon, and who carries out the instructing of those who, though few in number, seek a church marriage or the baptism of their children.

Other than on these "legitimate" occasions, the discourse of religion is a matter of extreme marginalisation in materialistic societies such as those in the United Kingdom and Australia. Even in the extremely "religious" atmosphere of the United States, religion has been marginalised, most notably through the recent scandals involving a number of fundamentalist television preachers. As a consequence both of these widely-reported scandals, and prior to that the secularisation of western societies, anyone attempting to discuss matters of theology or personal religious experience in any other context is likely to attract perhaps ridicule, perhaps abuse, but much more probably sheer lack of interest. More and more those who ignore religious traditions, but who feel quite free to express opinions on any other belief system (political, philosophical, theoretical) are embarrassed and even angered by any attempt to raise religious issues. It may well be the case that well-meaning fundamentalists impose on manifestly uninterested people in public squares, shopping malls and the like, and that such unmannerly

12

behaviour does not assist the cause of religion. But the anti-religious feeling in society at large is much deeper than merely a sense of outrage at violated privacy. It is part of a process of secularisation which in turn seems to have been accelerated by the endless crises of fear to which persons of this century have been subjected: fears of war, fears of nuclear holocaust, and fears of either nuclear winter, the greenhouse effect, the dissolution of the ozone layer, or all three.

Most telling of all, the roles of the elder, the priest and the wise woman seem to have been lost in western societies. It may be that the population at large looks to its political leaders for fulfillment of these roles, but if that is so, the results must be extremely disappointing. What can be seen, however, is the rise of the "author guru"; whether the book concerned deals with losing weight from hips and thighs, or methods of reconstructing one's psyche through meditation and carrot-juice, the role of the author is the same and the procedure which ensues is ritualistic-television interviews, book signings, seminars and other publicity stunts. This may all seem to constitute fantasy in and of itself, but it seems to me that what is happening in these secular situations merely images rather poorly what fantasy literature has achieved and is still achieving, the creation of author-priests whose role is to minister hope to readers and to construct visions of a reality in which humanity might transcend itself.

The notion of the author-priest has two important implications in this discussion. It raises the issues of the Romantics, particularly Wordsworth and Coleridge, but also, if peripherally, Shelley, on the role of the poet. Fantasy also is more often than not polemic, and authors of fantasy are often practising as "prophets of nature" in their appeal to the emotions and the imaginations of their readers. There is some distancing here from the claims of deconstructive theorists, in that there is very clearly something or someone "outside the text." Fantasy offers an affirmative metaphysics (the creation of new worlds, complete with intrinsic value systems, laws and customs), so that it can be seen, perhaps, as a new Romanticism.

For Wordsworth, the priestly function of the poet was determined by the faculties of the Imagination and of Memory. In his lengthy autobiographical poem *The Prelude*, Wordsworth shows how these faculties focus upon "spots of time," idealising them and imbuing them with moral and spiritual meaning. In other words, what happens is that Imagination and Memory reconstruct the past into a new world, a world with some relationship to mundane reality, but neither in nor of it. As Stephen Prickett has noted,

> The aesthetic importance of...Wordsworth gazing down into the mingled weeds and reflections from [his] boat is now clear. The very chameleon receptivity of the mind that had defeated the empirical philosophers is exploited as a source of poetry and growth. (89)

Prickett goes on to say elsewhere that while Coleridge attempted to establish a rapport with nature, Wordsworth tried to read into nature a particular moral message (160). Perhaps the best known example of this is found in the account Wordsworth gives in *The Prelude* of his adventure in the stolen boat, when he suddenly became aware of "a huge peak, black and huge" looming above the lake. This peak takes on a moral significance: it

> Towered up between me and the stars and still
> For so it seemed, with purpose of its own,
> And measured motion, like a living thing
> Strode after me. (1:382-85)

Of course one bears in mind the pantheism of the early Wordsworth, and certainly pantheism influenced his view that

> One impulse from a vernal wood
> May teach you more of man,
> Of moral evil and of good
> Than all the sages can. ("The Tables Turned")

But although the "impulse from a vernal wood" might be imbued with moral significance, it remained for the poet to make that significance known to others. To that end, Wordsworth records an initiation of a quasi-religious kind, complete with the assumption of a modern-day cloak of Elijah:

> I made no vows, but vows
> Were then made for me; bond unknown to me
> Was given; that I should be, else sinning greatly,
> A dedicated Spirit. (IV:334-37)

These lines seemingly allude to the practice of dedicating children to the Lord's service, as in the case of the Old Testament prophet Samuel, who was promised and dedicated to God before he was born, and taken to the temple as soon as he had been weaned (1 Samuel 1). Having been "dedicated," Wordsworth then assumed a prophetic ministry:

> ...to the open fields I told
> A prophecy: poetic numbers came
> Spontaneously to clothe in priestly robe
> A renovated spirit, singled out

Such hope was mine, for holy services. (1: 50-54)

If Wordsworth saw the poet as both prophet and priest, as these lines make clear, Coleridge does not so much empower the imagination as "baptise" it. The Imagination, for Coleridge, is "shaped" by Joy, and joy, although an "inner" quality, is not an innate one. Joy is a conditional gift, imputed to none "Save to the pure and in their purest hour"; but it too works upon the elements of nature to give them life and meaning. As Coleridge writes in his "Dejection: An Ode" (78-82), joy is

> ...the sweet voice, Joy the luminous cloud,
> We in ourselves rejoice!
> And thence flows all that charms or ear or sight
> All melodies the echo of that voice
> All colours a suffusion from that light. (71-75)

Recalling Coleridge's definition of the Imagination as comprising the faculties of perception and re-creation, it is clear then that without joy, perception is impaired. Without perception, there is no possibility of exercising the creative function. The lament of "Dejection: an Ode" is that joy has fled, leaving the poet without the ability to apprehend fully the beauty of the elements of nature; he can perceive, but he cannot receive:

> And still I gaze—and with how blank an eye!
> ...
> I see them all, so excellently fair;
> I see, not feel, how beautiful they are. (30: 37-8)

Wordsworth, too, believed that joy was a necessary precondition of exercising the priestly function of the poet. Without it, the poet is powerless to apprehend the meaning of nature, the divine message in all being:

> I feel the imaginative power
> Languish within me; even then it slept,
> When pressed by tragic sufferings, the heart
> Was more than full; amid my sobs and tears
> It slept, even in the pregnant season of my youth. (VII: 468-72)

It seems, then, that for these two poets the operation of the priestly or prophetic powers of the poet/author is conditional upon the acuteness of the poet's perception, which is dependent upon the inner state or mood of the poet. Without joy, it is impossible to perceive and recreate: in other words, it is impossible to write. Now of course this is a simplification of the two poets' extremely complex and various views, but it encapsulates, I think, something of the essence of what they believed in relation to their calling and their art. While Shelley makes no metaphysical claims for poetry, he does affirm that "Poets are the unacknowledged legislators of the world" (Shelley 448), attributing to the poet/author almost as much influence and power in this sense as Wordsworth and Coleridge do in their more traditionally mystical apprehension of the poet's role.

Twentieth century fantasists hold views cognate with and supplementary to such Romantic ones. C.S. Lewis, for example, began to write Science Fiction and Fantasy only after he had discovered what new worlds were "good for" in the rather ghoulish and ghastly novel by David Lindsay, *Voyage to Arcturus*. Imagined planets did not merely provide locations for all manner of *"Boy's Own"* adventures; rather they had a spiritual significance. Lewis wrote as follows of his discovery of the ulterior purpose in Lindsay's book:

Unaided by any special skill or even any sound taste in language, the author [Lindsay] leads us up a stair of unpredictables. In each chapter we think we have found his final position; each time we are utterly mistaken. He builds whole worlds of imagery and passion, any one of which would have served another writer for a whole book, only to pull each of them to pieces and pour scorn on it. The physical dangers, which are plentiful, here count for nothing, it is we ourselves and the author who walk through a world of spiritual dangers which makes merely physical dangers seem trivial. There is no recipe for writing of this kind. But part of the secret is that the author (like Kafka) is recording a lived dialectic. His planet, Tormance, is a region of the spirit. He is the first writer to discover what "other planets" are really good for in fiction. (Lewis, "On Stories" 35)

To create worlds in which readers find themselves drawn into a "lived dialectic" is to adopt, as author, a priestly, if not quasi-divine, role. Both Lewis and Tolkien held this elevated view of the role of the author, and both held that consequent upon this role was the almost religious experience of engaging with a text. Tolkien, for instance, pursued Coleridge's notion of the Imagination, claiming for the author (especially the author of Fantasy) the function of the Secondary Imagination, which Tolkien called "Subcreation." The most succinct expression of this belief is found in Tolkien's poem "Mythopoeia" which was addressed "to a man who described myth and fairy-stories as 'lies' ":

'Dear Sir,' I said—'Although now long estranged,
Man is not wholly lost nor wholly changed.
Dis-graced he may be, yet is not dethroned,
and keeps the rags of lordship once he owned:
Man, Sub-creator, the refracted Light
through whom is splintered from a single White
to many hues, and endlessly combined

in living shapes that move from mind to mind.
Though all the crannies of the world we filled
with Elves and Goblins, though we dared to build
Gods and their houses out of dark and light,
and sowed the seed of dragons—'twas our right
(used or misused). That right has not decayed:
we make still by the law in which we're made. ('On Fairy Stories' 49)

Applying this notion of the human right to "Subcreation," Tolkien argues the traditional Christian viewpoint that humanity, created by God in the image of God, will "inherit," as it were, the creative attributes of God, albeit on a finite plane. As Humphrey Carpenter notes, for Tolkien the making of myth and fantasy is an activity of subcreation and therefore a fulfillment of God's purpose, revealing a reflection of "a splintered fragment of the true light" (Carpenter 43). Language has special power over readers, Tolkien suggests, pointing out that etymologically the word "spell" means "both a story told and a formula of power over living men" (Tolkien 56). It follows then that the "spell" of imaginative Subcreation has a particular power over readers, opening up for them insights into divine truth.

That Lewis fully endorsed this view is seen is Lewis's own definition of myth:

Myth...is not merely misunderstood history (as Euhemerus thought) nor diabolical illusion (as some of the Fathers thought) nor priestly lying (as the philosophers of the Enlightenment thought) but, at its best, a real though unfocussed gleam of divine truth falling on human imagination. (Lewis 138n)

Something of Lewis's appropriation and adaptation of Tolkien's ideas can be seen from his late work of literary criticism, the book which he intended as a response to the Cambridge Leavisites among whom he found himself after his appointment, in 1953, to the Chair of Medieval and Renaissance Literature at Cambridge University. The book, titled *An Experiment in Criticism*, was never the significant contribution to criticism that perhaps it deserved to be; its timing, in the climate of critical change, was perhaps unfortunate, and yet it fits without discomfiture in the tradition of semiotics, emphasising the role of the reader and the active participation of reader with text. Moreover, it scorns the notion of a literary canon; Lewis had never venerated the notion of a "great tradition" as his own catholic tastes make clear.

In *An Experiment in Criticism*, Lewis offers the notion that literature has two constituent elements. It is both something *said* and something *made*. Developing this theory, Lewis makes plain his debt to Tolkien, and beyond Tolkien to Coleridge. As *something said*, literature is *Logos*, something which "tells a story, or expresses an emotion, or exhorts or pleads or describes or rebukes or excites laughter"; as *something made*, it is *Poiema*, "an objet d'art, a thing shaped so as to give great satisfaction" (Lewis, *Experiment* 132). The imaginative process of Subcreation inspires both categories of literature, so that the experience of reading provides, not the negative activity of "suspending disbelief," but the positive effect of self-transcendence, of escaping the confines of our own psychological boundaries. But it may be argued that this experience is not achieved without some tension between the two aspects of literature. The artistic form, *poiema*, may suppress or dominate the message, the emotional content, the *Logos*; the balance between them is delicate and if the equilibrium between them is disturbed, both may well fail to offer readers the experience of self-transcendence; a self-reflexive text may well work against it. Nevertheless, Lewis believes that the experience of reading arises out of a desire for self-transcendence: "We want to see with other eyes," he suggests, "to imagine with other hearts, as well as our own" (137).

There is, then, as Lewis sees it, a mutually enhancing process at work in the symbiotic relationship of *Logos* (itself a provocatively theological term) and *Poiema*, in the kind of writing which deepens readers' perceptions of the created world. One might extrapolate from Lewis's beliefs here the idea that through the operations of Coleridge's Secondary Imagination in poets and authors, readers are able to experience and enhance the operation of the Primary Imagination. Certainly reading is not a mundane activity for Lewis, but rather a transcendental and quasi-religious one:

> But in reading great literature I become a thousand men and yet remain myself. Like the night sky in the Greek poem, I see with myriad eyes, but it is still I who see. Here, as in worship, in love, in moral action, and in knowing, I transcend myself; and am never more myself than when I do. (Lewis, *Experiment* 141)

Of course, it is easy enough to argue that Christian writers such as Lewis and Tolkien would necessarily develop a critical approach to writing which would have elements of divine mystery about it, and that for such writers the role of author as priest would be hardly a revolutionary development but one which would arise naturally out of a system of theology to which they adhered. That might be so; but it does not explain the fact that other writers see the role of the author in very much the same way. Kurt Vonnegut, Jr., hardly a theological writer, claims for authors a priestly role in that they must provide consolation for readers in a meaningless world; this is the gist of his grimly amusing novel *Cat's Cradle*. It is a theme which recurs in Peter Beagle's gravely funny novel *A Fine and Private Place*, and again in his *The Last Unicorn*. It is hinted at in James Thurber's sardonic vignette "A Unicorn in the Garden," and given more concrete expression by Ursula Le Guin in

her incisive essay "Why are Americans Afraid of Dragons?" Le Guin
writes:

> Fantasy is true, of course. It isn't factual, but it is true. Children know that. Adults
> know it too, and that is precisely why many of them are afraid of fantasy. They know
> its truth challenges, even threatens, all that is false, all that is phony, unnecessary, trivial
> in the life they have let themselves be forced into living. They are afraid of dragons,
> because they are afraid of living. (44)

The neat distinction between "fact" and "truth" which Le Guin has
drawn here has some significant implications for determining the role
of the author. The author of fantasy is, at least implicitly, the author
of "truth"—someone who can mediate to readers the truth about life,
expose the shams of daily existence, and admit them to something—
to use Lewis's words—that will help them to "transcend themselves."
Le Guin is not a Christian; if anything she is a Taoist, but she affirms
in pretty nearly the same kinds of language the priestly function of the
author. And this affirmation is, I think, also implicit in the works of
Fantasy writers such as Russell Hoban, Susan Cooper and Madeleine
L'Engle, and indeed (as I hope to show in later chapters) of George
Orwell.

The quasi-divine function of the human imagination is also
recognised by Wilson Harris, who writes that in the broad reach of the
mythic impulse there is an

> ...art of a universal genius hidden everywhere in the...mystery of innovative
> imagination that transforms concepts of mutuality and unity, and which needs to appear
> in ceaseless dialogue between cultures if it is to turn away from a world habituated to
> the pre-emptive strike of conquistadorial ego. (Harris 137)

For Harris, "The voice of authentic self is the complex muse of otherness"
(*loc cit*). This is indeed power of some magnitude: the idea is that the
reach of the human imagination can break down cultural barriers, and
recreate human relationships and apprehensions of the world. It is an
authorially imputed textual power recognised although strenuously
denied by postmodernist critics.

The thrust of postmodernist criticism, especially that which falls
under the general heading "deconstruction," denies any role at all for
the author. The author is dead, as Roland Barthes wrote with some
glee in 1968:

> Writing is that neutral, composite, oblique space where our subject slips away, the
> negative where all identity is lost, starting with the very identity of the body writing.
> No doubt it has always been that way. As soon as a fact is *narrated* no longer with a
> view to acting directly on reality but intransitively, that is to say, finally outside of any

function other than that of the very practice of the symbol itself, this disconnection occurs, the voice loses its origin, the author enters into his own death, writing begins. (168)

Other theorists have hastened to approve of this critical stance, including Foucault (198) and Derrida (158). But can this view not be seen as somehow expressing, albeit in radically different language, the same kind of transcendence of self to which Lewis, Tolkien and Le Guin refer? I think it can. For what one must remember about the priestly role, at least as it is perceived during rituals and ceremonies, is that the *person* who fills that role, is, in a sense, "dead," or at the very least irrelevant. What matters is the ritual, the ceremony, the "text" as it were, of the functions of the priest, not his own thoughts, feelings and senses. There is a very real sense in which a priest officiating at a religious ceremony is hardly a person at all, simply a functionary. It may be that this is the role of the author, and that the notion of deferral to which deconstructors are committed is enacted in some sense by priests in their religious capacity, when their role, rather that their person, is emphasised.

And deconstructionist critics have adopted the model of the priestly role for the gurus of their philosophy. Although as an author he does not exist, Derrida's name is invoked in a quasi-religious sense; as indeed are such names as Foucault, Barthes, Hillis Miller and de Man. Indeed in one sense it could be alleged that the *name* is the theory, since occasionally the simple mention of the name evokes all that is meant by the theory. Of course, this is perhaps merely a cavil, but the fact remains that much deconstructive criticism invokes the names of theorists as authorities; and this practice, quite apart from the metaphysical nature of the theories themselves, reinforces the notion that authors have a function outside their personal selves, and this function is cognate with that of the priest. Such a statement, as I am aware, overlooks much of what has been said and written in deconstructive theory, but what has been said and written nevertheless always refers to the gurus, the priests, the functionaries whose final authority has been invoked. In this practice, it might be argued, deconstructionists are as traditional as any other theorist; nevertheless, it can be seen how the practice of deconstruction serves to illustrate the point about the priestly role of the author in the twentieth century.

If, as I suggested in Chapter One, there has been a displacement of religious discourse into the literature of fantasy, it is hardly surprising that one should also find that there has been something of a displacement of the role of priest into that of the author, particularly the author of fantasy literature. If fantasy literature is the voice of hope in this age of discontinuity, displacement and despair, then the authors of fantasy mediate that voice so that the readers can engage with it and experience, through the regeneration of their own imaginative faculties, the rebirth of hope. In this context, Coleridge's concept of the Imagination as a quasi-divine faculty has particular importance, not only for the author-priest, but also for the reader. Fantasy demands an active engagement by the reader with the text, so that perhaps one can think of the text/reader as a discrete entity, since each such engagement will produce different readings—even if only in minor details.

What then of sceptical texts? We have spoken of fantasy as the vehicle of "truth" if not of fact; but this seems to leave little room for the experience of valid doubts, of the rejection of religious forms and formulae. But this is not the case. Fantasy is, I suggest, the literature of hope, not of faith. Faith is not necessarily the most important element of religious experience. In any case I doubt whether it is the foundational element. Religious belief begins with hope, and the tentative reaching out of most humans towards religious beliefs of whatever kind appeals to them has its origins in hope: hope that things will change, that things will get better, that pain will be eased and sorrow healed. Indeed hope lies at the heart of most human relationships—a statement I make experientially rather than theoretically. It is hard to quantify such an assertion, but the imperative at the heart of most human actions is hope. One only has to listen to conversations throughout any given day to hear the word "hope" arise in any number of contexts. Human relationships fail, not because love is lacking but because hope has been lost. Fantasy works to restore hope, even in the most sceptical texts, as I intend to show. And I intend to show too that even texts which have long been regarded as affirmations of invincible religious faith have an intrinsic scepticism. It is too easy, I suppose, for critics to read into texts what they want to see. Many critics have looked at the texts I have selected and seen in them a triumph of faith. I have been looking for scepticism, for doubt and disbelief. I have found them, but it came as something of a surprise to me that I should discover also the articulation of hope.

The reason that I have used this approach is a simple one. In his book *Textual Power and the Teaching of English*, Robert Scholes examines Ursula Le Guin's *The Left Hand of Darkness* and shows (successfully, I think) how Le Guin is using her text in a subversive, indeed a "deconstructive" way. Of course, fantasy is as Rosemary Jackson has pointed out, "the literature of subversion," but Scholes takes pains to show how Le Guin carefully subverts and undermines conventional notions of sexuality and gender roles. He does not attempt to fit Le Guin into the role of the programmatic deconstructor, but, he says, "she is working in the same space, for many of the same ends, and having a good deal of success" (Scholes *Textual* 15). It occurred to me that fantasy might have other deconstructive purposes; that it might in some way undermine the scepticism of the current age and replace it with something which could sustain the human spirit. If that were so, then there is some cogent power behind the popularity of fantasy in both books and films; a power which mediates through works of fantasy a rebirth of hope. To offer consolation, healing and hope is, of course, a primary priestly function in religious practice; it is also one of the most potent functions of the literature of fantasy.

It might be said that it is also the role of the priest to undermine, subvert, and deconstruct apprehensions of the world and perceived reality, in order to draw attention to the unseen world of the supernatural. The activities are very close; as Susan Handelman has pointed out in her seminal work *The Slayers of Moses*, Christianity itself has undermined and subverted the Old Testament traditions of the Jews. An example is Christ's Sermon on the Mount, where on issue after issue, he deconstructs the "letter" of the Jewish law with his own formula: "It is written...*but I say*" (emphases mine). This is, I believe, the "formula" (if there is one) behind the creation of fantasy literature. It is part of the priestly function of author to create, through parable and precept, visions of how human existence ought to be. It uses, like the writings of the world's scriptures, metaphor and analogy, allegory and parable, to make moral points. Most of all, in its best and most sublime forms, fantasy fulfills the deepest and most heartfelt of human needs, the hope that the future will be better; that, indeed, there will be a future.

Chapter Three
Tolkien and *The Lord of the Rings*

*...For those with no faith, it's a way of finding
God again, and without challenging their unbelief...It
can be very comforting for people of my generation, who
ate disappointment for breakfast, lunch, and dinner.*

Umberto Eco, *Foucault's Pendulum* 236

Since the issues with which we are dealing—scepticism, faith and hope—are mostly commonly associated with Christianity, at least in Western societies, it seems appropriate to examine in the first instance two Christian authors who have had—and are still having—a profound influence on twentieth century fantasy. J.R.R. Tolkien was, by conversion, a Roman Catholic; he, with other colleagues, influenced the conversion to Christianity of C.S. Lewis (Carpenter 39-45). Lewis, however, became an Anglican; it has been speculated that perhaps the childhood influences of his Ulster Protestantism played a part in his decision to join the English church (Carpenter 51). Nevertheless, on some key theological issues, it is apparent that the views of the two men are congruent if not exactly the same, and it is also apparent that both men used their writings in various ways to provoke readers into an apprehension of the supernatural, of the claims of God upon humanity.

Lewis, of course, writes polemically; he knew the tactics of argument, dialectic and rhetoric, and he exercised his skill throughout the entire range of his writing. The first work he published after his conversion was *The Pilgrim's Regress*, a work so energetic in its attacks on the ideologies and beliefs which Lewis abhorred (not necessarily because of his conversion to Christianity) that he felt constrained to apologise for it ten years later in the foreword to the third edition of the book. Lewis is better known, however, for his so-called "Space Trilogy," the novels *Out of the Silent Planet, Perelandra,* and *That Hideous Strength.* Of these, the first one could be classified as a "space" adventure; the other two are very clearly spiritual thrillers. To be sure, *Perelandra* is set on the planet Venus, but only for the purposes of reconstructing certain elements of John Milton's epic *Paradise Lost.* All of these are, quite overtly, pieces of Christian polemic which have been, as I have

23

argued elsewhere, encoded strategically in metaphorical and symbolic language.[1]

Tolkien, on the other hand, used fantasy more covertly; religious themes are to be found in his best-known work, *The Lord of the Rings*, but they operate almost subversively, without detracting from the autotelic nature of the quest epic itself. Tolkien denied that his work could be read allegorically; but since he seems to be referring in particular to the way readers interpreted his orcs, Nazgul and arch-villain Sauron, as references to Nazi Germany (Carpenter 193), the allegorical correspondences he denied seem to be fairly narrow ones. It is possible to use the term "allegory" in a much broader sense and to read *The Lord of the Rings* as a representation of the way in which Tolkien perceived the human condition. Such a reading takes account of Tolkien's religious beliefs, without insisting on one-to-one correspondences with elements in the mundane world.

These two authors provide an interesting study of the way in which Christian believers reveal certain tensions in their faith; indeed both reveal in their fiction a scepticism which they seem unable to express elsewhere. C.S. Lewis's blithe dogmatism as read in the "space" trilogy seems to have taken a battering in the early 1950s, since two books from that period reveal scepticism, questioning and doubts of a deep and troubling kind: *Till We Have Faces*, Lewis's final adult novel, and *The Last Battle*, the final book in the children's sequence, *The Narnian Chronicles*. Since both these books also contain reworkings of themes found elsewhere in Lewis's fictional *oeuvre*, they provide a useful focus for analysis in the present context.

The Lord of the Rings, however, is all too often seen only as an affirmation of faith; the sceptical elements are often disregarded. But when one measures, as it were, the fantasy against Tolkien's seminal critical essay "On Fairy Stories," one is faced with certain incongruencies which raise probing questions about the absolutism of belief.

One of the interesting peripheral factors associated with the rise of post-structuralist criticism is the way in which it stimulated a rush by opposing critics to defend absolutism. To every hypothesis offered by the post-structuralists, absolutist critics would respond less with a rational rebuttal than with a howl of painful rage. Bruce Edwards Jr., in his insightful account of C.S. Lewis's literary theories (*A Rhetoric of Reading: C.S. Lewis' Defense of Western Literacy*), takes the opportunity to question the value of the theories of Saussure, Derrida and Stanley Fish; while my own essay, "Of Lunacy and Laundry Trucks," (1986) published in the 1989 issue of *Literature and Belief*, is similarly outraged. (In fairness, it should be noted that both Edwards and I have moved from our respective previous positions; in our different approaches, each of us has found much of value in those theories.) Such responses were due, I suggest, to a fundamental misunderstanding of what the post-structuralists were offering and not to a basic disagreement about the nature of the cosmos. For theories by very definition are not absolute in themselves. Scientific theories about the universe, for example, have changed radically in the last twenty years—not once, but many times. And still the best answer to questions about the universe is simply "We are not sure." Literary theories also rise and fall, since they constitute enlightened *questions* about the world, not answers. It is because absolutist critics are accustomed to absolutist answers that they find it difficult to accept theories which self-reflexively emphasise their own theoretical basis, postulating nothing more than a grandiloquently worded apology for literary agnosticism.

What has become apparent, however, is that the questions post-structuralist critics are asking about the world and the place of literary texts are not new. They have been part of a tradition of heterodoxy and scepticism over centuries, and indeed such writers as Lewis and Tolkien often ask the same kinds of questions. The essential difference between writers who hold some kind of religious belief and those who do not, is not a matter of faith—for faith is, as believers know experientially, a shaky and unreliable thing—but hope. And Tolkien and Lewis, in their best works of fantasy, articulate hope in a way that other authors have sought to emulate. Hope may be undefined, but it is more likely to be a source of comfort for the reader than a dogmatic assertion of faith. Fantasy provides no systematic theology, but it does give readers insights into possibilities; and in those possibilities lies the key to the growing popularity of the *genre*.

Because Tolkien's essay "On Fairy Stories" ostensibly states his position on the nature and function of fantasy, and because it was written while Tolkien was at work on *The Lord of the Rings*, it is worth noting some of the key elements in it, and using them as a basis to analyse the extent to which Tolkien was constrained by them in his practice. "On Fairy Stories" was originally delivered at St. Andrews University as the Andrew Lang Lecture, in 1938. The very fact that the lecture was a memorial to a great collector of fairy and folk stories undoubtedly determined the subject of the lecture; but Tolkien was by that time also well known through the publication of his children's story *The Hobbit* (1937), which has all the elements of a fairy tale.

Tolkien attempts, in the course of his essay, to define fairy stories, and to schematise what they offer to their readers. In doing so, he observes that myth, fantasy and religion have become "inextricably entangled"; even then, and even to him, the displacement of religious discourse into fantasy had become apparent:

Something really 'higher' is occasionally glimpsed in mythology: Divinity, the right to power (as distinct from its possession), the due of worship; in fact 'religion.' Andrew Lang said, and is by some still commended for saying, that mythology and religion (in the strict sense of that word) are two distinct things that have become inextricably entangled, though mythology is in itself almost devoid of religious significance.

Yet these things have in fact become entangled—or maybe they were sundered long ago and have since groped slowly, through a labyrinth of error, through confusion, back towards re-fusion. (28)

It seems clear, then, that Tolkien believed that the slippage of religious discourse into fantasy was in fact a restoration of both religion and myth; this point is made again, perhaps more cogently, in the poem "Mythopoeia" addressed to C.S. Lewis and included without identifying Lewis in this essay. The impulse humans feel to create "gods and their houses" in fantasy is an echo, or "form" in Platonic terms, of the creative impulse of God. That being the case, it would not be surprising to find that fantasy has especial power for both its readers and its writers.

As well as having this relationship with religion, fantasy provides a certain fulfilment for its readers through the experiences of Escape, Recovery and Consolation. Escape, Tolkien writes, is not a term to be used with scorn or pity, as it is in some critical circles; rather, the term describes not "the flight of the deserter" but rather "the Escape of the Prisoner." Fantasy gives us the opportunity to escape to the "real" world, to catch visions of the marvellous and the wonderful, to produce in turn the experience of Recovery.

Tolkien described one kind of Recovery in terms of Chestertonian Fantasy—seeing in trite and ordinary things a momentary glimpse of the weirdness and wonder of an alien world:

And there is (especially for the humble) *Mooreeffoc*, or Chestertonian Fantasy...It is Coffee-room, viewed from the inside through a glass door, as it was seen by Dickens on a dark London day; and it was used by Chesterton to denote the queerness of things that have become trite, when they are seen suddenly from a new angle. (52)

This approach, however, has only a limited virtue; Tolkien prefers fantasy that gives "luminosity" to simple elements in the Primary World, allowing his readers to share the experience he records of "[divining] the potency of the words, and the wonder of the things, such as stone, and wood and iron; tree and grass; house and fire; bread and wine" (53). And this last, of course, relates directly to the relationship between fantasy and religion.

This relationship is perhaps made more clear in the third of the experiences to which, according to Tolkien, readers are admitted through fantasy: Consolation. Fairy stories appeal to the imagination, and in the release of archetypes there is certainly a sense of consolation. But what Tolkien focuses upon is "the Consolation of the Happy Ending":

"Almost I would venture to assert that all complete fairy-stories must have it" (60). This consolation depends upon the fortunate turn of events, the "sudden, miraculous grace" that brings about the resolution of the story. Interestingly, this consolation is not that of *faith* as might be supposed; it is the consolation of *hope*:

> [Eucatastrophe] does not deny the existence of *dyscatastrophe*, of sorrow and failure: the possibility of these is necessary to the joy of deliverance; it denies (in the face of much evidence, if you will) universal final defeat and in so far is *evangelium*, giving a fleeting glimpse of Joy, Joy beyond the walls of the world, poignant as grief. (60)

It is easy enough to dismiss Tolkien's claims here as religious "pie in the sky by and by"; but some modified version of such a simplistic expectation lies at the heart of all expressions of hope. Nevertheless, trite and pretentious as it might seem expressed in this way, hope nevertheless is the imperative from which human existence springs. The ancient writers of the Christian scriptures recognised this; modern psychotherapists recognise it too, so that schools of therapies develop ways in which clients are able to feel "empowered," to produce "positive self-talk" and so on. All these devices are simply ways of injecting hope into an otherwise despairing existence. Fantasy offers hope—offers, as Umberto Eco's character observes in another context in the epigraph to this chapter, "ways of finding God without endangering disbelief." This is what makes *The Lord of the Rings* the seminal work of twentieth century fantasy, and as cover blurbs attest, the touchstone for all other fantasy since.

How Tolkien achieves the articulation of hope in the three-volume epic is both provocative and compelling, since he does it by seeming to concentrate on the forms of evil. In the early editions of the trilogy, the cover design featured a malevolent black eye—presumably the eye of Sauron. The title, too focuses upon evil—the "Lord of the Rings" is the evil lord Sauron. Past the title page, and the reader encounters the dark and tragic epigraph, "One Ring to rule them all, one Ring to find them,/ One Ring to bring them all and in the darkness bind them." The sonorous tone of these lines itself is an intimation of evil.

Chapter One, set in the Shire, a rather complacent region so far seemingly untouched by evil, uses language which is bright, almost an echo of the language of *The Hobbit*; but under the brightness there is the suggestion of menace: "At ninety-nine they began to call him *well-preserved*; but *unchanged* would have been nearer the mark" (33). Other words and phrases in the first few paragraphs which carry an intimation of menace include: "shook their heads"; "too much of a good thing"; "unfair"; "It isn't natural"; "trouble will come of it."

It is very clear from these opening lines that the Shire has not escaped the touch of evil. To be sure, the evil which pervades the Shire is obviously of a petty and unremarkable kind. It involves gossip, backbiting, jealousy, self-righteousness and greed. In the case of Bilbo, we see an unmistakeable desire to show off—not merely in his disappearing trick with the Ring, but in the very act of throwing himself a sumptuous party. It is his farewell to the Shire; one imagines it is a farewell to friends as well as to those who looked at him askance. Seen in its true light, the party seems to be a singularly nasty kind of farewell, as the various messages accompanying the gifts Bilbo leaves behind bear witness.

John Strugnell has noted, in a short piece titled "The Forms of Evil in The Lord of the Rings" (15) that the presence of evil in the Shire at the beginning of the book is personified more or less by Lobelia Sackville-Baggins, who has been pilfering spoons from Bilbo over a long period of time, and who, faced with an accusation in Bilbo's farewell message, attached to a case of more spoons, "took the point at once, but she also took the spoons" (50).

Although the Shire is undoubtedly "infected" by the evil abroad elsewhere in Middle Earth, it is true that the pettinesses practised there occur among genuine acts of friendship and kindness, as exemplified by the Gaffer and Sam Gamgee, Pip and Merry, and Hobbit practices generally—including the giving of *Mathoms*, or useless gifts distributed by anyone who was celebrating a birthday. Bilbo's gifts, although accompanied by acerbic remarks, are gifts nevertheless, offered in accord with the Shire's traditions.

This chapter illustrates very well Tolkien's theological understanding of the nature of evil. For him, as for most orthodox Christians, evil is not an absolute, the opposite of good; rather it is a "second level" corruption of the Good. God alone is good; God creates, and immediately his creation has choice—whether to serve the Creator, or whether to serve his or her self. According to Christian tradition, the first of the created beings were angels, and of them one elected to serve himself, becoming Satan, cast out of heaven by another angel, Michael. Satan and Michael are the opposed equals; God remains above them both. Evil in Christian thought, then, can always be overcome, since God alone (and therefore good) is absolute. But overcoming evil is not a matter in which God intervenes; it is left to the creature to make right choices. Tolkien does not allow us a *deus ex machina* to put things right; had he done so, there would be no epic. Tolkien selects instead a small hero, a "little man," and refers to him constantly as a "halfling." From this we might conclude that, metaphorically, Frodo is not only "small" in that he possesses a humility and meekness, but also that his need and greed for power will be less than that of the full sized human. There is a touch of real humility in his reluctant volunteering to take and destroy the Ring; all his "littleness" is embodied in his words, "I will take the Ring...though I do not know the way" (288). Frodo is pitted against great evil, and in the end he succumbs to it. But he is not condemned for that; the deeds of mercy and pity he has done in the past, and those of Bilbo as well, are what save him. Frodo's heroism is achieved by constant small well-meant deeds, not by the great achievement of destroying the Ring. But he is feted as though both kinds of achievement are equally heroic.

In the success of the "little man," the insignificant, ordinary human can take hope. Great deeds are not called for to effect redemption; rather all that one needs is the exercise of Pity and Mercy, qualities capitalised in the text which suggest their personification, from which might be extrapolated the existence and operation of the otherwise never-identified Deity of Middle Earth. Tolkien provides, in the breadth of his mythic creation, a sense of wonder and terror which reinvest the mundane world with an awe-arousing majesty. Whether one beholds distant hills and towers, or is simply left amid the primeval potency of the forest, the magic of Middle Earth is always mediated for us through the hobbits, and for them through the ancient nature spirits which have lain undetected in their lairs—the Balrog, the Shelob, the Ents, the Barrow-wights, Tom Bombadil. These ancient entities are beyond the reach of the Ring's power, but act according to their natures which have been determined by choices made long ago. Other mediators are, of course, Gandalf the wizard and Strider, both of whom have beneficent missions of guidance and empowering. The hobbits, away from the mundane setting of the Shire, learn to experience wonder even in the midst of danger. At the beginning of the journey there is the succour of elves, but even at the very foot of Mt. Doom, Sam's great wish is fulfilled as he sees the Oliphaunts.

And it is perhaps because Tolkien manages to lighten the darkest moments with glimpses of wonder, to fill the bleakest hours with jokes about herbs in the Houses of Healing, that it is difficult to accept the conclusion to the epic as truly consolatory, whether to Sam Gamgee upon whom the curtain closes, or to the reader. Sam has seen Frodo and Bilbo off to journey with the Elves to the Grey Havens; he returns to home and hearth, to his wife and small daughter. There are two troubling issues here.

The Grey Havens seem to correspond to some degree with the notion of the wondrous isles in the West described in the Irish legend of Hy-Brasil. Indeed, Tolkien had this myth in mind as he wrote *The Lord of the Rings*, because he mentions it in "On Fairy Stories" (13). Hy-Brasil has some correspondence with the Isles of the Blessed, or the classical notion of Elysium, a place to which the souls of the thrice born are consigned.[2] In *The Lord of the Rings*, the Grey Havens cannot be a heavenly or paradisal realm; for one thing the setting is post-lapsarian and pre-redemptive, and for another the colour "grey" betrays them. Gandalf is "the Grey" before his self-sacrificial act at the Bridge of Khazad-Dum, and afterwards is apotheosized into "the White." The "Grey" Havens, then, are less than Paradise, which would be, according to Tolkien's moral lexicon, "white." Because Tolkien was a pre-Vatican II Roman Catholic, he would also have access to the doctrine of Limbo, a place or state of happiness wherein dwelt the souls of those good persons who died before Christ effected redemption. It was from Limbo that these souls were liberated after the death of Christ. Limbo was also said to be the dwelling place for unbaptised babies; it was a happy place, but without the perfect happiness of the Beatific Vision. So this ending is not quite the happiest that it might be for Frodo and Bilbo; that, we might assume, is yet far off in the future.

As for Sam, Merry and Pippin, who return to the Shire and prosperity, the consolation is also a limited one. The Shire has been scoured, and evil no longer reigns there; nevertheless it is not the same Shire that the Company left. This is the Shire whose days are numbered as the Age of Men is dawning, and it is a Shire which is still mundane reality, with its emphasis on commerce, government and domesticity. Sam has seen elves and oliphaunts: there seems, to me at least, some correspondences here with the fate of Sancho Panza in Cervantes' novel *Don Quixote de la Mancha,* who returns to his wife after the death of his master. There is no doubt that Sam loves his wife and his daughter, and no doubt that he is pleased to be with them. But his "Well, I'm back," seems to be a sigh not only of relief, but also of regret.

Adventures, at least in this world, cannot go on forever; and one must return to mundane reality. While I take Tolkien's point that one returns from enchanted lands with the recovery of a sense of wonder, he does not successfully depict recovery here. If present, it is in a form much diluted and diffused; there is a touch of what C.S. Lewis would call *Sehnsucht* haunting the final scene of the novel. The effect of this is that the element of Consolation, the *pre-evangelium* of which Tolkien speaks in his essay, is severely militated against. This is a necessity in a plot which is concerned with the gradual degeneration of nature brought about by the Fall, and which is set in a time when the hope of redemption is a distant and faint one—so faint, in fact, that there are, apart from symbolic figures such as the Elves, no images of religious practice in the book.[3]

This is a surprisingly sceptical stance for an author who was a staunch Roman Catholic. The lack of even the slightest intimation of some kind of religious practice, or even of the benevolent interest of a Deity, suggest in Middle Earth a certain agnosticism which seems to undermine and subvert, indeed one might even say "deconstruct," the affirmations

Tolkien makes in "On Fairy Stories." It is true that Tolkien preferred to keep his religious polemic to a minimum, and he was said to dislike C.S. Lewis's Narnian Chronicles because of their intrusive and insistent Christian imagery (Carpenter, *J.R.R.T.*, 233-34). But even in *The Hobbit* there is no suggestion of a religious message. It may be that Tolkien has chosen only to hint at the supernatural; and hints, certainly, are there, in the magic of Gandalf and his mysterious return as the apotheosized "White" wizard, and, as David Lake has pointed out, in the many coincidences and hairsbreadth rescues which occur in the trilogy (20-25). Nevertheless, the metaphysical approach of *The Lord of the Rings* is, for many Christians, a surprisingly negative one, and some fundamentalist groups have "read" into the trilogy all manner of evil, sceptical, or even demonic messages.[4] But if *The Lord of the Rings* does not present a ringing apologetic for Christianity, it does offer the articulation of hope for a readership extending across the boundaries of belief. While Christians might be heartened to find their faith defended in a popular work such as this one, the wider benefit might well be that all readers might be encouraged to hope that they might share with the "Little Human," Frodo, the qualities of Pity, Mercy, humility and endurance which contribute to the success of the quest. And the deepest and most enduring hope of all is, of course, that as evil rises in every age, there will be a "wayfaring Christian," as Milton wrote in his *Areopagitica*, to take up the cause of good.

Tolkien suggested, after all, that fantasy should be *"pre-evangelium"* and not outright evangelism. In refusing to make his major work an overt apologetic, he exhibits a belief shared by C.S. Lewis that the writer of fiction is dishonest if what he passes off as fiction is really a sermon. While Lewis is far more polemic in his early fiction, however, his last novel, *Till We Have Faces*, shows something of the same restraint as *The Lord of the Rings*, and indeed is the most sceptical novel in Lewis's fictional *oeuvre*. It, like Tolkien's epic, is the story of a quest, but while it also offers at times a sense of wonder, there is in it also deep soul searching, despair and anguish which make for extremely painful reading. Perhaps that is why it remains Lewis's least popular novel. To my knowledge no critic has seen in it any correspondences with Tolkien's *The Lord of the Rings*, but the analysis in the following chapter will, I hope, show that they exist and that they have some relevance to the articulation of hope in an age of increasing despair.

Chapter Four
C.S. Lewis Saves Face

Nought gold where your hair was;
Nought warm where your hand was;
But phantom, forlorn,
Beneath the thorn,
Your ghost where your face was.
Walter de la Mare

In the United States in particular, there has developed around both Tolkien and Lewis a cultic fascination, encouraged, no doubt, by the publishers of books about them. There has been a particular emphasis upon Lewis as a right-wing reactionary, a patron saint of fundamentalist religion and ideologies.[1] Lewis's stepson, Douglas Gresham, has spoken out on several occasions against the "plaster saint" image which has been constructed around Lewis.[2]

Certainly a glance at the range of Lewis's literary *oeuvre* would suggest that he was a Christian of absolutist beliefs. He published, as well as his fiction, an extensive range of popular theological works, some of the most important of which were based upon his radio talks. But when one looks at the views Lewis expressed before his conversion to Christianity, one sees there the same absolutism. Lewis was a man of very strong beliefs, and many of these were retained after his conversion; indeed it could be said of him that he converted to Christianity because Christianity accommodated the beliefs he already held. For example, his antagonism towards coteries or "inner rings" is made very plain in a letter he wrote to Owen Barfield in May, 1928, when he complained bitterly about the situation in his college.[3] And as early as 1919, Lewis wrote to his father about his abhorrence of coteries (*Letters of C.S. Lewis* 48).

Similarly, Lewis's reputed misogyny, given religious sanction in such essays as "Priestesses in the Church?" (*God in the Dock* 238) has its origins in his youth when, according to Margaret Hannay, he wrote "with glee" of the "good omen" that the number of "wimmen" at Oxford was to be limited (Hannay 19). As I have noted elsewhere, many, indeed most, of the views which Lewis expounded as a Christian apologist were part of his world view long before he was converted. This is not to say, however, that he was insincere; the fervour of his writings stems very clearly from a commitment to strongly held beliefs; my point is simply that these beliefs can be differentiated from Lewis's Christian faith. So when one turns to his final novel *Till We Have Faces*, and reads that the idea had been "thickening and hardening" in his mind since his youth, it is important to bear in mind that Lewis's beliefs did not in fact constitute his faith, and that as with Tolkien and *The Lord of the Rings*, *Till We Have Faces* reveals something of the author's scepticism.

Till We Have Faces is a novel which betrays its author's spiritual and emotional pain. Humphrey Carpenter has written that it is autobiographical, a point taken up by critic Peter Schakel, and I think there is good reason for that assumption (Carpenter 256, Schakel 151). Not only do most of the theological themes which Lewis addresses elsewhere in his fiction appear, but also some of the problems he experienced in his own spiritual development. Douglas Gresham claims that his mother, Joy Davidman, had a considerable influence on this novel, working on it in 1956 and 1957 (Filmer 380). But there is an error in these dates, and although Lewis knew Davidman prior to the publication of the book in 1956, they were not yet married. This is not to say that the book does not reflect the influence of the friendship that had developed between them. Lewis's portrayal of the female protagonist suggests that he felt much empathy with her; and perhaps this empathy was achieved, in part, through his relationship with Joy Davidman. But those critics (for example, Green and Hooper 257-78, Carpenter 233-52, Hannay 15-20) who aver that *Till We Have Faces* represents a marked change in his attitude to women take little account of the other female characters in the novel. Indeed it can be argued that the narrow range within which Lewis categorised women determines the nature of all his female characters in this book as in all his fiction, and indeed in all his writings. There is the goddess (Psyche), the warrior-queen or Amazon (Orual), the slut (Batta), and the sexually predatory Redival. Cognate characters can be found in the range of Lewis's of other fiction.[4]

Readers expecting to find from Lewis in his final novel a ringing affirmation of his Christian faith are often disappointed. It is worth noting that *Till We Have Faces* is the least popular of Lewis's works. There have been a number of scholarly attempts to rehabilitate the novel as an affirmation of Lewis's faith,[5] but there has been very little recognition of the scepticism which lies behind the narrative. A book which begins with the words, "I am old now and have not much to fear from the anger of the gods" (11) and concludes with a parenthesized account of a manuscript that ends in meaningless lines (320) can hardly be said to be an affirmation of great and absolutist faith. The ending, by Lewis's previous standards, is extremely unsatisfactory; the narrative is self-reflexive and the closure is problematical. This, I believe, is the reason that Lewis's usual readership, Christians with a deep commitment to their beliefs, find the novel not to their liking. Readers who feel alienated by absolutist beliefs will, however, find much to identify and to empathise with in this novel. It is a tortured, questioning novel, full of doubts, fears, and terrors; but it offers, if not reassuring absolutism, at least (albeit faintly) the articulation of hope for the individual.

If Lewis exhibits a sceptical slant in this novel, it is hardly surprising. After all, he was profoundly influenced by the works of George MacDonald, and later, by his friendship with Charles Williams. Both of these writers wrote in the sceptical tradition; both of them were heterodox, not only in their beliefs but also in the way they encoded their beliefs in their writings, owing a great deal to the Hermetic tradition, to Gnosticism and Neoplatonism, and to the writings of William Blake.[6] An example of the scepticism and doubt in MacDonald's work can be seen in the extraordinary ending to *The Princess and Curdie*:

> Irene and Curdie were married. The old king died, and they were king and queen. As long as they lived Gwyntystorm was a better city, and good people grew in it. But they had no children, and when they died the people chose a king. And the new king went mining and mining in the rock under the city, and grew more and more eager after the gold, and paid less and less heed to his people. Rapidly they sunk towards their old wickedness. But still the king went on mining, and coining gold by the pailful, until the people were worse even than in the old time. And so greedy was the king after gold, that when at last the ore began to fail, he caused the miners to reduce the pillars which Peter [Curdie's father] and they that followed him left standing to bear the city, and from the girth of an oak of a thousand years, they chipped them down to that of a fir tree of fifty. (255-56)

One day, when life was at its busiest,

> the whole city fell with a roaring crash. The cries of men and the shrieks of women went up with its dust, and then there was a great silence.
> Where the mighty rock once towered, crowded with homes and crowned with a palace, now rushes and raves a stone obstructed rapid of the river. All round spreads a wilderness of wild deer, and the very name of Gwyntystorm has ceased from the lips of men. (256)

This fatalistic and somewhat gratuitous postscript to MacDonald's conventional fairytale ending raises some searching questions about what the author intended. Certainly it subverts and undermines Tolkien's notion of eucatastrophe and the happy ending (at least as far as earthly existence is concerned), setting up in its place a vision of destruction and desolation. It seems to echo Shelley's bleak commentary on human power in his poem "Ozymandias," and, for a Christian of supposedly great faith, it seems to be a very pessimistic view of the world. But it is not only a tragic world view which is at work here; it is also a sceptical view of the traditional fairytale ending which shows the ultimate triumph of Good over the forces of evil. The idea of the happy ending is, according to Tolkien, consistent with Christian eschatology; but MacDonald does not point beyond the desolation of Gwyntystorm to a future "new heaven and new earth."

Nevertheless, MacDonald's story does articulate hope, although the hope it offers is on the individual plane, not the social or the global. Hope, it would seem, depends upon individual choices which have consequences, not merely for the individual but for the society of which that individual is a part. Curdie's right choices deliver Gwyntystorm from the malaise which infects it, and they bring prosperity and happiness to the city while it remains under his reign. After his death, the welfare of the city depends on the choices of its ruler. MacDonald's judgment upon individuals is harsh, but in its very harshness is the element of hope, not merely for the individual but for the society of which he or she is a part. Nevertheless, in this view hope is a fragile thing, and it is very clear that it rests upon moral choices.

Lewis deals with this issue of choice in *Till We Have Faces*, as he confronts his character Orual with issues of faith and doubt, and since Orual is the queen of her country, her choices will determine the fate of her subjects. Lewis takes pains to show the effects of service to Orual in close-up, focusing on those who have been close to the queen— her sisters, her tutor, and her chief soldier, Bardia. Orual succeeds only in destroying them in various ways and to various degrees. It is left to Bardia's wife to confront Orual with her devouring and destructive choices:

...Faugh! You're full fed. Gorged with other men's lives; women's too. Bardia's; mine; the Fox's; your sister's; both your sisters'. (275)

The allusion here is clear; Orual is psychologically and spiritually a vampire. It is a realisation which Orual must make for herself:

'I am Ungit.' My voice came wailing out of me and I found that I was in the cool daylight and in my own chamber. So it had been what we call a dream. But I must give warning that from this time onward they so drenched me with seeings that I cannot well discern dream from waking nor tell which is truer. This vision, anyway, allowed no denial. Without question it was true. It was I who was Ungit. That ruinous face was mine. I was ... that all-devouring, womblike, yet barren, thing. Glome was a web; I the swollen spider, squat at its centre, gorged with men's stolen lives. (287-88)

This passage makes Orual's vampiric nature quite clear, but there are also correspondences between this "bloated Spider" image and Tolkien's gruesome monster the Shelob, with whom Frodo and Sam battle in the bleak days before their arrival at Mt. Doom:

There agelong she had dwelt, and evil thing in spider-form, even such as once of old had lived in the land of the Elves in the West... How Shelob came there, flying from ruin, no tale tells...she served none but herself, drinking the blood of Elves and Men, bloated and grown fat with endless brooding on her feasts...for all living things were her food.... (Tolkien, LOR 750)

Lewis's goddess Ungit, and by association Orual who identifies with her, are quite clearly drawn from the same archetypal image as Shelob. This is the image of Lilith, who, according to Jewish legend, was Adam's first wife. Lilith sought power, and despite her overwhelming and devouring sexuality, was unable to have children. She refused to allow Adam to copulate with her, since she would not allow him the superior position. Enraged, Lilith flew to the lands about the Red Sea, where her behaviour was uncontrollably promiscuous, and Midrashic legend has it that she retains the power to harm or kill infants, and she is sexually predatory upon men who are alone in a house by night (Patai 182-184). It is not surprising, then, that the use of this archetype by both Tolkien and Lewis relates closely to its use by MacDonald, whose Lilith in the novel of the same name is a vampire, using her sexual charms to exploit and dominate Mr. Vane in the supernatural domain. The correspondences between Orual and Lilith are emphasized by the fact that both are redeemable, and by the continuing discourse in both novels on the nature of their spiritual experiences—are they, perhaps, only dreams?

This is of course, an adaptation of the philosophy of Bishop Berkeley (1685-1753). Berkeley believed that *ideas* are the only things which have "real" existence, and that material things exist only through perception (Berkeley 27-50). In the novel *Lilith*, MacDonald plays games with the issues of dream, reality, and illusion; and it is not surprising to find him quoting from Novalis in both his adult fantasies, *Lilith* and *Phantasies: "Unser Leben ist kein Traum, aber es soll und wird veilleicht einer werden"* ("Our life is no dream, but it ought to become one, and perhaps it will"). But to decide whether something is an illusion or dream, or reality, is to make certain choices about the nature of faith and belief. These are the issues at stake in *Till We Have Faces*; the book is an extended discourse upon the nature of belief as revealed through visions, revelations and dreams.

In this respect, it has a great deal in common with Charles Williams' novel *The Place of the Lion*. C.S. Lewis was deeply influenced by this novel, to the extent that he wrote a "fan letter" to Williams expressing his delight with it (Carpenter 99). When Williams came to Oxford during the war years with the University Press, Lewis pursued the friendship and Williams became part of the Inklings, despite Tolkien's less than heartfelt welcome. In *The Place of the Lion*, Williams's thesis seems to be something very close to William Blake's aphorism from *The*

Marriage of Heaven and Hell, "Without Contraries is no Progression." Certainly the plot of the novel progresses through the tensions between faith and disbelief as expressed through the experiences of the characters Damaris Tighe, Quentin Sabot and Anthony Durrant.

It is hardly surprising that scepticism should be a feature of Williams' work, since, as John Heath-Stubbs points outs, Williams' existentialism and "Christian scepticism" were major components of his transcendentalist philosophy. Williams believed that scepticism was not antithetical to faith; in other words, he followed the tradition of fideism, the notion that scepticism leads ultimately to faith (Douglas 374). For Williams, as Heath-Stubbs writes, disbelief means the human need, and even the right and duty, to question. Heath-Stubbs adds that in his theological work *He Came Down from Heaven*, Williams "characteristically lays emphasis on Mary's question to the angel" after hearing the message of the Annunciation: "How shall these things be?" (14).

The effectiveness with which Williams raises the issues of belief and scepticism in *The Place of the Lion* depends upon the way he uses the element of incalculability to produce *frissons* of fear and awe which provide the reader with a sense of the numinous. And in this novel the use of incalculability is very close to the Deconstructionist device of aporia, whereby readerly expectations are displaced, subverted or contradicted. The novel opens, for example, with two men on a quiet country hike, waiting for a bus to take them home, when they are warned about the presence in the area of an escaped circus lioness. The expectation aroused here is that the men will be in some way threatened by or confronted with the physical reality of the lioness, but in fact what they see is the lioness being absorbed by a huge lion. In other words the physical entity of the lioness has been replaced in the men's experience by the Platonic ideal of Lion-ness. The action takes place in the evening, when the men's vision is none too clear, and the rest of the opening chapter consists in an ongoing dialectic on the nature of what they have seen, as shown in the following passage:

'...it wasn't a lion,' said [the leader of the search party]. 'There's been no lion in these parts that I ever heard of, and only one lioness... What d'ye mean—lion?'

'No,' said Anthony.... 'Of course, if there wasn't a lion—I mean...O well, I mean there wasn't if there wasn't, was there?'

But a few seconds later, resuming his journey with Quentin, Anthony speaks to himself: "But, damn it!... it *was* a lion." (14)

The rest of the novel carries on this kind of dialectical discussion between vision and reality, with each seeming certainty undermined by some intrusion from the world of the unseen. Although Williams subverts readerly expectations in his proto-Deconstructionist use of aporia, his approach is quite unlike that of Derrida, who has written that he does not believe anything like perception exists ("Structure" 272); Williams does not undermine so utterly the validity of perception. Williams, though sceptical, never approaches nihilism; rather he pursues through his idiosyncratic use of aporia a progression, through Contraries, to the hope of spiritual individuation through apotheosis.

Lewis does something very similar in *Till We Have Faces*. Although Lewis does not imitate Williams' style (for which present-day readers should be profoundly grateful, since Williams's prose style is extremely turgid as the quotation above reveals), there is no doubt that Lewis has, consciously or otherwise, taken up the notion of a dialectic between faith and scepticism. Lewis also avoids nihilism; his character Orual questions the gods, and seeks answers from them; she never doubts they exist. What she doubts is their beneficence, their role in her affairs, and her need to capitulate to them. She doubts, too, the notion of supernatural intervention in her affairs; her visions, she reasons, are illusions. Lewis has constructed this novel very carefully; the inconclusive closure and the self-reflexivity of the text (it is *about* writing a complaint to the gods, and in parts is highly meta-narratological) means that readers can engage with the text and construct what they will of meaning and significance. It is a difficult task for hermeneutical analysis, which is possibly why it receives such perfunctory treatment from a number of critics; but it raises some of the same questions as Tolkien's *The Lord of the Rings*.

For example, both books are concerned with quests, and in both books the questers are offered guidance, with varying degrees of success. Frodo, though in many ways a "little person," nevertheless does not pass up a chance to show off at The Prancing Pony, even to the extent of using the Ring as a means to pull off a rather childish disappearing trick; and in the episode just prior to the appearance of the Gollum at Mt. Doom, Frodo's pride has become full-blown from his over-use of the Ring and his proximity to the power of the Dark Lord. Frodo becomes arrogant, and will not destroy the Ring:

'I have come,' he said. 'But I do not choose now to do what I came to do. I will not do this deed. The Ring is mine!' And suddenly, as he set it on his finger, he vanished from Sam's sight. (581)

There is something uncomfortably similar in Orual's behaviour as it is exhibited early in Lewis's novel. Her possessiveness is obsessional:

...I see the boughs always rocking and dancing against blue-and-white skies, and their shadows flowing water-like over all the hills and valleys of Psyche's body. I wanted to be a wife so that I could have been her real mother. I wanted to be a boy so that she could be in love with me. I wanted her to be my full sister instead of my half sister. I wanted her to be a slave so that I could set her free and make her rich. (31)

The novel is very clearly a tale of gradual self-knowledge, of discovering the "Ring" of self-absorption in the nature of the protagonist. Like Tolkien in *The Lord of the Rings*, Lewis finds it useful to employ Jungian imagery, or at least, the kind of proto-Jungian imagery one finds in George MacDonald's *Lilith*, through which to explore the deepest motivations of the human soul. Orual has a "shadow" in the dark and bloody goddess Ungit, and she must confront her shadow. This she does after her visit to Psyche's home with the God of the Grey Mountain, when, following the myth of Cupid and Psyche from Apuleius, Psyche reluctantly gives in to her sister's request and holds up a lantern in order to see her husband's face, an act which has been expressly forbidden her.

Orual watches from a distance. When Psyche lights the lantern, there is a great sound of thunder, and around Orual a dazzling light as the god confronts her:

A monster—the Shadowbrute that I and all Glome had imagined—would have subdued me less than the beauty this face wore. And I think anger (what men call anger) would have been more supportable than the passionless and measureless rejection with which it looked upon me. (181-82)

The god is silent, but in that look is a penetrating accusation:

...he rejected, denied, answered, and (worst of all) he knew, all I had thought, done or been.... He made it to be as if, from the beginning, I had known that Psyche's lover was a god, and as if all my doubtings, fears, guessings, debatings, questionings...all the rummage and business of it, had been trumped-up foolery, dust blown in my eyes by myself. (182)

Despite this terrifying judgment, however, the god is not angry; he gives Orual the promise of hope: "You, woman, shall know yourself and your work. You also shall be Psyche" (*loc. cit.*). But even in this hope is a terrible promise. The achievement of self-knowledge is agonisingly painful, and it is only through the pain of self-recognition that Orual can finally face herself and know herself. As in the original myth, she has been set tasks of an exceedingly difficult nature, but in them she is aided by Psyche, or so she dreams. Eventually, Orual is brought to self-renunciation, able to face Psyche in a dream of the Deadlands, and saying, "Oh Psyche, oh, goddess,...Never again will I call you mine; but all there is of me shall be yours..." (317). As she renounces her self, the god appears: "You also are Psyche," he says in a great voice (319).

It seems to me that the act of self-renunciation after completing a quest, a series of tests, as it were, is similar to Frodo's quest in *The Lord of the Rings*. There is good reason for concluding that the Ring of Power is something like the Original Sin, or in Catholic theological terms, the tendency to self-will and self-aggrandisement with which humanity, both collective and individual, is tainted as a result of the Fall. This sin must be purged from human nature before one can enter heaven; in *The Lord of the Rings* it is significant that the Ring is something to be destroyed. And while Original Sin is collective and universal, it is nevertheless the responsibility of the individual to deal with its effects in his/her own life. The Ring affects only the individual who is wearing it; Frodo's quest, although told as the adventure of an individual, has a universal quality. He is "Everyperson" who functions on behalf of all humanity in what amounts to an epic parable. The quest Tolkien relates operates in the reverse to traditional quest literature, in which some treasures must be found. But *Till We Have Faces* also details a quest to lose something—and that "something" is very close to the self-empowering, self-aggrandising, and self-deceiving Ring of Power. Orual, like Frodo, achieves her quest by losing the "self," and like Frodo she does so through the influence of someone else—not only her sister Psyche, the bride of the god, but also of those other characters who have worked in her life for good or for ill, including, in the latter category, her father, the goddess Ungit, and the slave Batta.

One of Lewis's early poems, published in his first post-conversion novel *The Pilgrim's Regress*, shows that the notion of self-knowledge and self-renunciation had been with Lewis for many years before he came to write *Till We Have Faces*; indeed it encapsulates the entire theme of the novel:

> Because of endless pride,
> Reborn with endless error,
> Each hour I look aside
> Upon my secret mirror
> Trying all my postures there
> To make my image fair.
>
> Then and then only turning
> The stiff neck round, I grow
> A molten man, all burning
> And look behind and know
> Who made the glass, whose light
>   makes dark, whose fair
> Makes foul, my shadowy form reflected there
> That self-Love, brought to bed
>   of Love may die and bear
> Her sweet son in despair.
>   (Lewis, *Regress* 184)

Interestingly, the same themes are reiterated in a very late poem, written to his wife shortly before her death of cancer:

> All this is flashy rhetoric about loving you.
> I never had a selfless thought since I was born.
> I am mercenary and self-seeking through and through:
> I want God, you, all friends, merely to serve my turn.
>
> Peace, reassurance, pleasure, are the goals I lack,
> I cannot crawl one inch outside my proper skin:
> I talk of love—a scholar's parrot may talk Greek—
> But, self-imprisoned, always end where I begin.
>
> Only that now you have taught me (but how late) my lack.
> I see the chasm. And everything you are was making
> My heart into a bridge by which I might get back
> From exile, and grow man. And now the bridge is breaking.
>
> For this I bless you as the ruin falls...
>   (Lewis, *Poems* 109-110)

The novel *Till We Have Faces* deals with the same kind of spiritual agony as that which is revealed in these two poems. In struggling with the difficulties of self-realisation, Lewis "accuses the gods" through his character Orual, who speaks with Lewis's voice throughout the narrative. It is because this novel is so haunted by the spectre of Lewis's self that those meaningless "marks" at the end become significant. The first part of the novel ends with the words, "No answer"; the penultimate paragraph of the second part takes up the theme:

> I know now, Lord, why you utter no answer. You are yourself the answer. Before your face questions die away. What other answer would suffice? Only words, words; to be led out to battle against other words. (320)

This is a subversive conclusion to the narrative. On the one hand, it offers assurance and comfort ("You are yourself the answer"), but on the other, it posits the alternative, the sceptical dismissal of the gods ("Only words, words; led out to battle against other words.") The affirmation of faith is not the conclusion; Orual was in the act of writing more, and we are not shown what that "more" might have been. It is difficult to see that Lewis has concluded the narration with a glorious affirmation of faith; it seems as though he is left with as many questions as he began with. Nevertheless, he does not deny hope to his readers. The narrative leaves the issue of belief open; but in Orual's dream experiences there is a measure of encouragement, a quantum of solace achieved through the articulation of hope.

This novel is very close in its patterning to Tolkien's *The Lord of the Rings*, although the issue of intertextuality is not immediately apparent, and to my knowledge has not been critically discussed before. But Tolkien's work has been so influential in this century that it is difficult to find a fantasy writer who has not been in some ways influenced by it. In the following chapter I shall discuss a trilogy with a frank debt to Tolkien, although it has been written from a radically different religious viewpoint. But, like Tolkien's trilogy, Ursula Le Guin's *The Earthsea Trilogy* is about human spiritual and psychological growth, and like George MacDonald's *Phantastes* and *Lilith*, and like Lewis's *Till We Have Faces*, it is about "good death," that is, the renunciation of self and of power and dominion over others. It offers no reassuring absolutism; but what it does offer, from a number of perspectives, is the articulation of hope.

Chapter Five
The Shadows of Earthsea:
Ursula Le Guin

...I will show you something different from either
Your shadow at morning striding behind you
Or your shadow at evening rising to meet you;
I will show you fear in a handful of dust.
                    T.S. Eliot, *The Wasteland*

Fantasy written for children has become increasingly sophisticated in the twentieth century. The avuncular tone of much Victorian children's literature is missing, and with it the rigidly prescriptive "happy ending." In C.S. Lewis's Narnian Chronicles, the separate stories end with a return from the marvellous to the mundane which amounts to something of an anticlimax and is often quite pessimistic, as in *Prince Caspian*, when Peter and Susan Pevensie are told that they are now "too old" to return to Narnia. The penultimate paragraph, which tells of their return to the mundane world, is decidedly anticlimactic: "It was odd, and not very nice, to take off the royal clothes and to come back in their school things (not very fresh now)...(194). They find themselves in the railway station (Lewis's preferred threshold for this series) feeling "a little flat and dreary." Peter exclaims: "Well... We *have* had a time." To which Edmund responds: "Bother!... I've left my new torch in Narnia" (194-95).

The Last Battle, with its grim and almost despairing opening phrase, "In the last days of Narnia," ends happily enough with the Beatific Vision of the transformed Aslan; but there is a certain sadness in his words: "There *was* a real railway accident... Your father and mother and all of you are—as you used to call it in the Shadow-Lands—dead... The dream is ended: this is the morning" (183). Lewis's point, of course, is that after death something much better awaits, especially for those who have been friends of Narnia. Nevertheless, to the spiritually unawakened reader, the tragedy of the accident and the deaths of an entire family could detract considerably from the paradisal after-death experience that Lewis, wisely, does not try to describe.

43

There is about the ending of Tolkien's *The Lord of the Rings* the same sort of tragedy. Sam, Pippin and Merry stand watching Frodo, Bilbo, and the Elves "going West." Of course, the "west" is associated with adventure and discovery, thanks to the American legends of heroism in its western territories. It also evokes recollections of the mystical and the marvellous, as in the legend of Hy-Brasil. But to servicemen during the two World Wars (both Lewis and Tolkien served in World War I,) "going west" was quite clearly a reference to dying. Tolkien's imagery combines all these notions; he,like Lewis, believed in some kind of spiritual afterlife which was rich with promise according to Christian concepts of heaven. Nevertheless, to Sam who of the three hobbits who remain in the Shire is the most sensitive, and to whom Frodo was closest, the departure of his friend has elements of tragedy.

The concept of tragedy always involves the idea of death, and despite conventional religious beliefs about the life beyond it, the very word evokes grief and pain. One of the traditional roles of religious discourse is to attempt to come to terms with the notion of death, to imbue it with promise and hope, to offer to the bereaved the consolation that the loved one is "not lost, but gone before." It is in connection with death that religious language attempts to convey hope. Today, however, while still predominantly religious, funerals are moving more and more into the realm of the secular as unbelievers eschew the rites of a religion in which they have never believed. Secularity may be honest, but the comfort it offers is necessarily limited.

Ursula Le Guin's rejection of Christianity means that she must attempt to come to terms with death in radically different ways, and since she is writing for young people, she is constrained by literary tradition to find some way of expressing her views within the context of a "happy" (or at least, "satisfactory") ending. Her Earthsea Trilogy, then, deals with death by focusing upon the Tao, in which the Yang and Yin pairings offer also the balance between life and death. Le Guin leads up to the final novel in the trilogy by introducing different aspects of death in the preceding books. First, her young wizard must learn to put pride to death and face his own Shadow; then the mature wizard is engaged in a struggle to help a young woman escape from the "death" of dogmatic and sexual repression; and finally, the ageing wizard must face the reality of his own death and accept that death is part of the Balance or Equilibrium by which the world exists and is sustained. In *A Wizard of Earthsea*, the young, proud Ged initiates his dealings with the realm of the dead by attempting to call up spirits, in particular the spirit of the legendary Queen, Elfarran. In doing so, Ged is dabbling in forbidden things, for although the dead can be called up by Mage magic, to do so as a game destroys the Balance.

For the Taoist, the Balance of Equilibrium constitutes the sacred, "the Absolute, the Unknowable Reality beyond all manifestation" (Gaskell 744); it is the organising and sustaining principle of the Universe. It is represented by the Yang-Yin symbol, and the pairing of opposites associated with either the Yang (male) or Yin (female) of which the best known are Left and Right, Light and Dark, Life and Death. Death, then, is essential for Life; and symbolically, putting to death the lust for power over others, escaping from the "death" of dogmatic repression, and facing death as part of life, are all ways in which Death paradoxically means Life for the Individual. In *The Earthsea Trilogy* Le Guin offers these three perspectives upon death. In doing so, she strives to achieve not the "pre-evangelium" of eucatastrophe suggested by Tolkien, but rather the portrayal of the personal wholeness and the heroism of humans who come to terms with the power and rhythm of the Universe. Moreover, in showing the experience of Death as something to be welcomed as part of life, and not to be feared or evaded by fruitless quests for immortality, Le Guin's fantasy clearly appropriates elements of religious discourse.

Where Tolkien shows us Gandalf, a wizard who has achieved much wisdom, and through self-sacrifice at the Bridge of Khazad-Dum becomes apothesized from "the Grey" into "the White," Le Guin takes her readers stage by stage through the development of Ged from his *enfances* in *A Wizard of Earthsea* to his eventual apotheosis in *The Farthest Shore*. Each stage in Ged's development is a kind of death. As a youth, an apprenticed Mage, he must put his pride to death, for it has been most unmistakably his pride which causes him to release his Shadow in the contest he stages with his *bête-noir*, Jasper. The Archmage, Nemmerle, saves Ged's life and in doing so loses his own—a model for what Ged must endure in the last stages of his own life (66). And the new Archmage, Gensher, tells Ged quite plainly that Pride has been the cause of the catastrophe which has torn the fabric of the world and released the Shadow which will dog Ged's existence until he is able to confront it. Gensher says,

...You have great power inborn in you, and you have used that power wrongly, to work a spell over which you have no control, not knowing how that spell affects the balance of light and dark, life and death, good and evil. And you were moved to do this by pride and hate. Is it any wonder the result was ruin? You summoned a spirit from the dead, but with it came the powers of unlife. Uncalled it came from a place where there are no names. Evil, it wills to work evil through you. The power you had to call it gives it power over you: you are connected. It is the shadow of your arrogance, the shadow of your ignorance, the shadow you cast.... (68)

It is quite clear from this passage that immortality as conceived by Christians forms no part of the Balance. Those who cling to immortality become the Undead, the Nameless ones, the source of the true evil by which the Balance can be disturbed. It is clear, too, that Ged's rite of passage through the experiences with his Shadow is essential to his mission in *The Farthest Shore*. He learns the importance of his true Name, not so much through the lectures he received from Ogion, his guardian, or the mages on the Isle of Roke, but from his confrontation with his shadow. Names and identity are a part of life, and are not lost in death if death is welcomed as part of life. Only when the proud and foolish cling to life is identity lost.

It is significant, then, that when Ged confronts his shadow he is humble enough to recognise it in the dark aspects of his own psyche and call it by his own name:

> Aloud and clearly, breaking that old silence, Ged spoke the shadow's name, and in the same moment the shadow spoke without lips or tongue, saying the same word: "Ged." And the two voices were one voice.
>
> Ged reached out his hands, dropping his staff, and took hold of his shadow, of the black self that reached out to him. Light and darkness met, and joined, and were one. (164)

In this moment of self-realisation and self-acceptance, Ged becomes psychologically and spiritually individuated: "...Ged had neither lost nor won, but, naming the shadow of his death with his own name, had made himself whole" (165-66). Of course in this novel as in the other two which complete the trilogy, there are resonances of Coleridge's Ancient Mariner, who endures Death-in-Life until he is able to face his guilt and atone for it by loving and accepting the creatures in the sea about him. Ged, too, while being pursued by his shadow has, symbolically, an "albatross" about his neck; only by facing it and accepting it as part of himself does he truly achieve Life-in Life. Moreover, in *The Earthsea Trilogy* there is no concept of "winning" or "losing"; rather the emphasis lies on self-acceptance and harmony with the rhythms of the universe, a concept radically different from the notion of good winning over evil which is such a feature of Western literature derived from the Judaeo-Christian scriptures.

If there was any doubt that Le Guin regards Christian belief with utmost scepticism and even a degree of scorn, her point of view is very much in evidence in the second novel of the trilogy, *The Tombs of Atuan*. Indeed, the religion of the God King is as dogmatic, cruel and rigid as that of Orgoreyn in *The Left Hand of Darkness*, where the religion of Yomesh, and its central city Mishnory, have distinct resonances of Christian terms such as the name Yeshua (Jesus Christ) and missionaries. Indeed, even the title of the Priestess, "the Eaten One," is reminiscent of the Eucharistic ritual in traditional Christian churches. Moreover, the region of the Tombs is a Waste Land, a spiritual desert which resembles a convent where dogma is enforced and there is little joy:

> The days went by, the years went by, all alike. The girls of the Place of the Tombs spent their time at classes and disciplines. They did not play games. There was no time for games. (185)

Arha, the Priestess, finds a childhood friend in another novice, Penthe, and together the two make for themselves some mild amusements in teasing some eunuchs who watch over them. But any violation of the rules will mean punishment, at least for Penthe, as Penthe well knows. Not only is this a realm of rigid dogma, it is also a sexless world. The only men the girls encounter are eunuchs, and as with every expression of gladness or joy, sexuality is severely repressed. The misery of the Priestess, despite her position, is made poignantly clear when the eunuch Manan finds Arha making her way to bed after the usual rituals, on the night when Penthe has been punished for their escapade in staying out after the curfew. Manan asks,

> 'Were you punished?'
> 'I can't be punished.'
> 'No... That's so...'
> 'They can't punish me. They don't dare... They can't touch me. I am Arha,' she said in a shrill, fierce voice, and burst into tears.
> The big, waiting hands came up and drew her to him, held her gently, smoothed her braided hair. 'There, there. Little honeycomb, little girl...' She heard the husky murmur in the deep hollow of his chest, and clung to him. Her tears stopped soon, but she held on to Manan as if she could not stand up.
> 'Poor little one,' he whispered... (193)

The priestess is, at this time, merely a child; but later as she matures, her duties include the sacrifice of those who have some way offended against the God King, and who have been imprisoned in the Tombs. There are, in the light of the other very clear references to Christianity, allusions, most probably deliberate, to the Inquisition and other church-backed atrocities in the description of this cruel and rather bloodthirsty practice. What Le Guin achieves here is a most effective undermining and deconstructing of the claims of traditional Christianity to offer any kind of solace or hope. Of course, it can be argued that there is historical verification for Le Guin's allusions, and it is true that behind many historical atrocities there has been, either directly or indirectly, some kind of church sanction. Nevertheless, even for Le Guin worship of the God King and making sacrifices to him is not the worst or only evil. There is in the priestess Kossil an even more potent evil, since she "had no true worship in her heart of the Nameless Ones or of the gods. She held nothing sacred but power" (220). While Thar, the strict, but kindly priestess was alive, there was a kind of equilibrium which held Kossil's worst impulses in check; with the passing of Thar, Kossil's jealousy of Arha becomes more fervid and intense, to the extent that she begins to plot Arha's death.

It is then that Arha ventures into the Tombs, ostensibly to sacrifice another intruder. But this intruder is different; he works sorcery. It is Ged, the Wizard. The story of Arha and Ged is a kind of reverse account of a Mary Magdalene; according to Christian belief, Christ delivers the Magdalene from the accusations of adultery, but Ged delivers Arha from the curse of sexual repression. As her relationship with Ged ripens, Arha learns to trust him, and he calls her by her true name, Tenar. Through Ged's wizardry, Tenar is set free from the imprisonment of the Tombs. Through his masculinity, she is set free from the sexual repression which has restrained her womanhood, although there is no hint of a physical relationship between the wizard and the girl. She experiences a kind of "death" (hence the title metaphor of the book); but it is death to repression, to dogma, and to slavery. These things are symbolically suggested by the Nameless Ones, who are not dead; as Ged tells Tenar, "They exist. But they are not your Masters. They never were. You are free, Tenar. You were taught to be a slave, but you have broken free" (266).

Tenar's freedom from the Tombs, then, articulates hope for all who are imprisoned by cruel and rigid doctrines, by blind dogma, by repression and lack of joy, since in emerging from the Tombs it is quite clear that Tenar is in some sense "reborn" or awakened; she emerges from the Waste Land into a Garden. Like Ged, and like Coleridge's Ancient Mariner, she too is delivered from Death-in-Life to individuation and freedom. Yet in the traditional fairy story, Tenar would marry her "prince." The Sleeping Beauty, once awakened, becomes a bride. So much is promised for Tenar, but her future does not belong with Ged. He has his own mission to fulfill, and this time his encounter with death is intensely personal.

The Farthest Shore begins, rather like Lewis's *The Last Battle*, with a bleak and pessimistic picture of disorder in the natural world. Le Guin applies the spider/vampire archetype to all humanity to illustrate the evil of human beings who do not venerate the Equilibrium:

'What are you watching there?' the Archmage asked, and the other answered, 'A spider.'

Between two tall grassblades in the clearing a spider had begun a web, a circle delicately suspended. The silver threads caught the sunlight. In the centre the spinner waited, a grey-black thing no larger than the pupil of an eye.

'She too is a patterner,' Ged said, studying the artful web.

'What is evil?' asked the younger man.

The round web, with its black centre, seemed to watch them both.
'A web we men weave,' Ged answered. (312)

The world is in chaos because the Equilibrium has been upset by mortals clinging to immortality. Ged responds to the call for help, and sets out on a journey to "the farthest shore" of Earthsea, and symbolically to "the farthest shore" which is death. He is accompanied by the young Prince Arren, who looks to Ged for heroism, leadership, and messianic magic. They sail westwards; like Tolkien, Le Guin exploits the same mythological icon of the "West." But time after time during their long journey, Arren witnesses the "failure of wizardry as a great power among men" (390). In Hort Town, all magic has failed. The people take refuge in drug-induced dreams and hover between death and life. Theirs is also a kind of Death-in-Life which is against nature and the Equilibrium. Arren senses there "not a presence of any quality but an absence, the weakening of all qualities, like a sickness that [infects the soul]" (347). Later, the disillusioned Arren broods upon the diminution of hope: "there was nothing in magery that gave a man true power over men; nor was it any use against death" (loc cit). When Arren, bored with the tedium of their journey at sea, asks Ged to use a spell to create a following wind, Ged's answer is "grudging, hard to understand":

There, thought Arren, lay the very heart of wizardry; to hint at mighty meanings while saying nothing at all, and to make doing nothing at all seem the very crown of wisdom. (390)

There is a subtle irony in Arren's resentful ruminations, since "doing nothing at all" is part of Taoist belief. As Taoist writer Benjamin Hoff observes, the "Bisy Backson" (a term taken from A.A. Milne's *Winnie the Pooh*) "thinks of progress in terms of fighting and overcoming... Of course, *real* progress involves growing and... changing inside" (104). Arren begins as a "Bisy Backson" who must learn the way of the Tao. It is a lesson Ged learned as a young wizard. Indeed, during his time of service on Low Torning in the first book of the trilogy, Ged tries to heal the son of Pechvarry, despite the lore he had learned from the Master Herbal at Roke: "Heal the wound and cure the illness, but let the dying spirit go" (80). Moved by the sorrow of the child's mother, Ged attempts to save the boy, but he pays the price of his well-intentioned folly, as he is drawn into the flight of the dying child's spirit and confronts his Shadow at the boundary of life and death. This is the lesson Ged keeps in mind, at least implicitly, as he journeys in *The Farthest Shore*, but it is a lesson Arren does not understand.

When Sopli, their companion, dies, and Ged makes no effort to save him, Arren's faith in Ged and magery is completely destroyed.

[Ged] had brought them into peril, and had not saved them. Now Sopli was dead, and he dying, and Arren would die. Through this man's fault; and in vain, for nothing.

So Arren looked at him with the clear eyes of despair and saw nothing. (399)

Bleaker yet is the encounter with Cob, the spirit who has conquered death and who hovers between the worlds. Through Cob's refusal to die, the Balance has been disturbed; in the choice of one being lies the fate of an entire world. Cob cannot recall his True Name; and even as he argues with Ged about the extent of victory over death, he forgets even his use-name. He is one of the Nameless Ones who lives between worlds. From the name he gives himself ("The Immortal One," "King," and "I who died and live") it seems quite clear that Le Guin is again taking issue with the central Christian doctrine of the Resurrection. Cob is a cruel parody of Christ as a blinded, helpless, nameless and gibbering wreck. The "salvation" offered by Ged is death. And in giving death to Cob, Ged is drained of his wizard's powers, since they are finite, and have not been imputed to him by any supernatural source. He is taken away by a dragon who rescues them from the shores of death, and the Doorkeeper of Roke observes, "He is done with doing..." (477).

The ending is ambiguous, although it is happy enough for Arren, who is made king. There are two possibilities which Le Guin explores before leaving the fate of Ged open-ended, but obviously one which is consonant with the values expressed in the book. It seems that although Le Guin is rarely classified along with Lewis and Tolkien as a didactic author, this work is highly didactic. Its relentless deconstructing of Christian beliefs, its continual preaching by various mages on the significance of Balance or Equilibrium, its occasional authorial intrusions on the nature of existence, all make this an exercise in fictional pedagogy. The undermining of traditional religious beliefs (in the Ressurrection of Christ, for example) is not new, nor is it something on which Le Guin holds a copyright, but it certainly adds to the scepticism and the pessimism of this trilogy.

In a world titled "Earthsea," there are close correspondences with this mundane world of earth and sea. And despite the scepticism of her text, Le Guin offers some hope for the world, achieved through the notion of harmony with the Universe, through "being" and not "doing," through the upholding of the Equilibrium by non-interventionist co-operation with Nature. The three novels of the trilogy are, in many ways, quasi-Romantic texts, with Le Guin's Taoism not far from the pantheism of the early Wordsworth. Certainly her treatment of Death-in-Life in each of the books is strongly reminiscent of Coleridge. In the troubles which beset Earthsea in the final novel, Ged notes that "Only in death is there rebirth. The Balance is not a stillness. It is a movement—an eternal becoming." (423). This concept is very close to that of the German Romantics, and of both Coleridge and Wordsworth, whose poetry has

been called "the poetry of growth" (Prickett *passim*). At the same time
the three books in *The Earthsea Thrilogy* are determinedly deconstructive
and subversive, challenging believers and non-believers alike to assess
their relationship with the world about them and also their relationships
with their fellow human beings.

Possibly where Le Guin offers the most concrete evidence of hope
for humanity is in her attack on the misuse of Power. She is, however,
careful to differentiate, at least implicitly, between the different
equivocations upon the word. Power as talent is the "raw material,"
as it were, which can be shaped by various forces with which it comes
in contact. The young Ged has the talent for the working of magic.
The misuse of Power is the domination over, and control of, other living
beings. Ged aspires to this kind of power, as seen in the early episode
in which he calls the goats, and in the disputes with Ogion, his guardian,
about the "uses" of things; and finally in the way in which he is first
by the little girl and finally by Jasper drawn into using his gift in a
contest, to prove his superiority. The third kind of power is that which
Ged must learn, and that is the power of self-discipline, the ability to
do nothing when nothing is the best thing to do. In that, at least, is
the articulation of hope; for of such restraint comes true heroism and
affection.

The themes which Le Guin addresses so cogently feature also in
fantasy films which use Jungian imagery by which to convey messages
of religious significance. For example, the *Star Wars* trilogy, while
following the form of the traditional fairy tale (the first film begins
with the words, "In a Galaxy, far far away..."), nevertheless has Luke
Skywalker confronting his Shadow in the form of Darth Vader. And
in an emotional scene in the final film, Vader is transformed by the
confrontation in an example of Jungian individuation. Moreover, the
deity invoked in these films is merely "The Force," surely a concept
not incompatible with Le Guin's Taoist "Equilibrium," itself a Force,
a breath, or a rhythm.

A further example of similar imagery can be found in *The Dark
Crystal*, as the viewer slowly becomes aware of correspondences between
the Mystics and the Skeksis, until they are drawn together under the
triple suns in a splendid moment of reunion and individuation into
the great, shining creatures who gather about the restored crystal. The
broken shard of crystal obviously symbolises the splitting of Light from
Shadow, and the great entities are restored in the same instant as the
crystal is made whole.

The popularity of such films as these, and their many imitators,
reveals a certain preoccupation with religious themes in modern cinema
which apparently takes its cue from similar developments in the literature
of fantasy. As Peter M. Lowentrout points out, fantasy critics are aware

of a "displacement [into fantasy] of religious concern and content" (346). Indeed, Lowentrout gives evidence gathered from surveys he has conducted into the reading habits and beliefs of children and young adults, that speculative fiction plays a major role in determining the religious outlook of its readers. There are, he admits, instances in which the connections between religion and fantasy are quite explicit; he cites the way the novels of C.S. Lewis support Christian orthodoxy and the novels of Marion Zimmer Bradley support feminist Neopaganism. But he adds,

> But of far greater importance for the religious formation of our times than these explicit connections between religion and areas of displaced religious concern and content is the way in which such areas, and especially speculative fiction, more generally work for the reenchantment of our world once more making real for many the fundamentalist assumptions upon which all specific religious belief rests. (348)

In other words, what Lowentrout is arguing is that through the operation of what J.R.R. Tolkien calls "recovery," that is, by refreshing the imagination and specifically the imaginative faculty of perception with the defamiliarising operation of metaphor and symbol, fantasy literature enables us to view the mundane world in a new light, seeing in it the wonders which caused the ancestors of humanity to make up stories about the existence of gods who created the world and its inhabitants, and who might be in some way involved in the determination of human destiny. In Le Guin's trilogy, Arren articulates for us all our expectations of the gods and the humans they empower, and if Ged (or God?) cannot deliver the goods, the result is despair; the loss, not of faith, but of hope. And because hope is the sustaining virtue, sustaining that is, even when love and faith have failed, Le Guin cannot ultimately deny her readers that. Her two endings, her suggestion that Ged now rules "A greater kingdom," measure her capitulation to the truth that readers need, demand, and are sustained by, hope. More importantly, whatever Ged's personal fate, he has restored the Equilibrium in Earthsea, so that it is a world now in perfect Balance. In Le Guin's religious lexicon, there is a hint of Blake's aphorism from *The Marriage of Heaven and Hell*, "Without Contraries is no Progression." Contraries, the series of opposites in Balance as the Yin/Yang circle symbolises, are the essence of the Tao. Balance, in particular the Balance between Life and Death, is essential to the harmony of the world, to harmony within the individual spirit, and to growth.

Possibly the most religious aspect of Le Guin's work—religious, that is, in a way that appeals to all her readers, and which mitigates the didacticism in her work—is in her view of the Imagination, a view not incompatible with that of Coleridge, although not entirely consonant with it. The purpose of the imagination (she does not capitalise it) is

"to give you pleasure and delight"; "imaginative fiction is to deepen
your understanding of the world, and your fellow men, and your own
feelings and your destiny." (*Language of the Night* 43) She goes on
to add in a much-cited passage, that many people fear fantasy because
"They know its truth challenges, even threatens, all that is false, all
that is phony, unnecessary, trivial in the life they have let themselves
be forced into living" (*Language of the Night*, 44).

Something of the same kind of philosophy and a similar attitude
to the imagination, although they are argued from a slightly different
perspective, appear in Russell Hoban's post-holocaust novel, *Riddley
Walker*. In the following chapter, I shall discuss the way in which Hoban
offers his readers the articulation of hope both in this novel and in his
children's book *The Mouse and his Child*, drawing some correspondences
between Hoban's acerbic humour, his droll pessimism and his search
for hope and meaning, and those of Lewis Carroll, of whose tradition
Hoban is a worthy follower.

Chapter Six
Walking Riddles and the Last Visible Dog:
Russell Hoban

'When I use a word,' Humpty Dumpty said, in a
rather scornful tone, 'it means just what I choose it to
mean—neither more nor less.'
'The question is,' said Alice, 'whether you can
make words mean so many different things.'
'The question is,' said Humpty Dumpty, 'which is to
be master— that's all.'
Lewis Carroll, *Alice Through the Looking Glass* (269)

If Lewis Carroll was the Elijah of riddling, then his mantle has fallen on the worthy Elisha of Russell Hoban. Like Carroll, Hoban uses riddles to ask searching questions about language and life, and like Carroll he imbues his comedy with pathos. Like Alice, Hoban's characters must traverse certain rites of passage, and in doing so achieve a measure of wholeness and contentment. This is not to deny a certain scepticism and pessimism in Hoban's work; there is no deliverance promised for the world or for western society. But on the individual plane, Hoban offers the hope of self-transcendence and spirituality, and he does this in both his adult fantasy *Riddley Walker* and in his children's novel *The Mouse and His Child*. I have chosen these books from Hoban's literary *oeuvre* because of the correspondence in their themes, and because of the different treatment of these themes for readers in different age groups.

Hoban's children's novel, *The Mouse and his Child*, tells the story of a quest undertaken by a wind-up toy in the shape of a father mouse and child mouse facing each other and clasping each other's hands. The story begins pleasantly enough with the mouse toy on display in a toy-shop with other wind-up toys, and dolls whose papier-mache heads are made from old newspapers. The dolls can only speak in fragments of the news, advertisements and commentary written on the pieces of paper from which their heads are made. One doll cries:

'Prices slashed... EVERYTHING MUST GO.'

An elephant, another wind-up toy, agrees:

54

'You're quite right,' said the elephant.

'Everything must, in one way or another, go. One does what one is wound to do. It is expected of me that I walk up and down in front of my house; it is expected of you that you drink tea. And it is expected of this young mouse that he go out into the world with his father and dance in a circle.' (17)

This, of course, sounds comfortingly deterministic; but fate goes terribly wrong. The mouse toy is sold, and eventually it is damaged and discarded. A tramp finds the mouse and his child during a forage in a trash can, inexpertly repairs the clockwork mechanism, and turns them out onto a highway to fare as best they can. First they are captured by the evil Manny Rat who exploits toys in his business of theft, blackmail and torture; but the Mouse and his Child escape. They find themselves in a Brechtian drama group called "the Caws of Art"—it is run by crows. The play in production is called *The Last Visible Dog*, and during a rehearsal the mouse and his child are inspired by the mystical resonances in the play to continue their adventuring to see "the last visible dog." As one of the characters says, there is "a jiggling and wiggling... Out among the dots beyond... Beyond THE LAST VISIBLE DOG!":

'It's getting me now,' said Mrs. Crow.

'But what does it mean?'

Crow flung wide his broad wings like a black cloak.

'What *doesn't* it mean?' he said. 'There's no end to it—it just goes on and on until it means anything and everything, depending on who you are and what your last visible dog is.'

'Beyond the last visible dog,' said the mouse child to his father. 'Where is that, I wonder?'

'I don't know,' said the father, 'but those words touch something in me—something half-remembered, half-forgotten—that escapes me just as it seems almost clear.' (68)

There is something of a spoof on the magic and mysticism that one finds in contemporary fantasy, and also upon some forms of religious practice. "Dog," of course, is an anagram of "God," a fact Hoban is careful to exploit again in *Riddley Walker*. Here the joke is limited to the familiar philosophy that God is what and where an individual wants him to be, an allusion perhaps, if a trifle oblique, to the claims of the Apostle Paul to being "all things to men." The suspicion that Hoban is here playing punning games with his readers is well founded, since we learn that what the Mouse and his Child ultimately discover is a tin can, half buried in mud at the bottom of a flooded stream:

Bonzo Dog Food, said the white letters on the orange label, and below the name was a picture of a little black-and-white spotted dog wearing a chef's cap and carrying a tray on which there was another can of Bonzo Dog Food, on the label of which another little black and white spotted dog, exactly the same as the first but much smaller, was walking in a tray on which there was another can of Bonzo Dog Food, and so on until the dogs became too small for the eye to follow. (109)

This passage has elements in common with the episode in Lewis Carroll's *Alice Through the Looking-Glass*, where a perpetually bemused Alice is confronted by the perplexing nature of reality. In trying to establish his own answers to the riddle of life, the universe and everything, Carroll draws from the theories of Bishop Berkeley (1685-1753). Berkeley believed that *ideas* are the only things which have "real" existence, and material things exist only through perception (Berkeley 52). It is this notion which Carroll takes up when Tweedledee and Tweedledum are made aware of the Red King's snoring:

'He's dreaming now,' said Tweedledee: 'and what do you think he's dreaming about?'
Alice said 'Nobody can guess that.'
'Why, about you!' Tweedledee exclaimed, clapping his hands together triumphantly. 'And if he left off dreaming about you, where do you suppose you'd be?'
'Where I am now, of course,' said Alice.
'Not you!' Tweedledee retorted contemptuously. 'You'd be nowhere. Why, you're only a sort of thing in his dream!'
'If that there King was to wake,' added Tweedledum, 'You'd go out—bang!—just like a candle!'
'I shouldn't!' Alice exclaimed indignantly. 'Besides, if I'm only a sort of thing in his dream, what are you I should like to know?'
'Ditto,' said Tweedledum.
'Ditto, ditto!' cried Tweedledee.
He said this so loud that Alice couldn't help saying 'Hush, You'll be waking him I'm afraid, if you make so much noise.'
'Well, it's no use your talking about waking him,' said Tweedledum, 'when you're only one of the things in his dream. You know very well you're not real.'
'I *am* real!' said Alice, and began to cry.
'You won't make yourself a bit realler by crying,' Tweedledee remarked: 'There's nothing to cry about.'
'If I wasn't real,' Alice said,—half laughing through her tears, it all seemed so ridiculous—'I shouldn't be able to cry.'
'I hope you don't suppose those are *real* tears?' Tweedledum interrupted in a tone of great contempt. (194-95)

Some aspects of this passage not only apply to the Alice books as a whole, but are also relevant to the themes Hoban develops in *The Mouse and His Child*. First, as Martin Gardner, who has annotated the book in scholarly detail, has pointed out, the Looking Glass story, like its companion tale of Wonderland, is an account of one of Alice's dreams, so that Alice is dreaming of the Red King who is also dreaming of her, like two mirrors facing each other. From this we might conclude that if there are two mirrors facing each other, there are an infinite number of reflections—Alice dreaming the king who is dreaming of Alice who is dreaming the King, and so on. Carroll gives us a picture of infinity, a picture captured with humour and insight by Hoban with his infinite parade of dogs.

A further correspondence between Hoban and Carroll can be detected when one considers Stephen Prickett's observations about this passage from Carroll; he writes:

> Just as Tweedledum and Tweedledee are mirror-images of each other, so Alice seems to have found *her* mirror image in the Red king (remember she is eventually going to be a White Queen). (Prickett 98)

Something similar occurs in Hoban's text. The mouse and his child are trapped in the ooze at the bottom of a flooded stream, where they meet C. Serpentina, a snapping turtle who responds to their urgent pleas to escape with philosophical absurdities, including some neat puns: "One has no need to get out of here... One sees below the surface of things. One thinks in depth and acquires profundity... Contemplation." When the mouse child asks what the turtle contemplates, he replies, "Infinity, mostly" (108). A few lines later, he indicates the dog food can and tells the mice, "...an endlessness of little dogs, receding through progressive dimunition to a revelation of the ultimate truth" (109). And the ultimate truth? After long days beneath the ooze on the bed of the stream, the mouse child beholds it. C. Serpentina has chewed the label from the can, and the mouse child sees his father and himself reflected in the mirrored surface of the shiny tin. Like Alice, the mouse child meets his mirror image in the experience of infinity (116). It is clear that in a sense both authors suggest that "the kingdom of God is within" the individual who is able to confront his/herself. Mirrors, one recalls, are Jungian devices in literature by which access is gained to the subconscious on the path to self-knowledge and individuation. While Carroll predates Jung, there is ample evidence (from, for example, the psychological fiction of George MacDonald) that the ideas Jung predicates had wide currency in the mid-nineteenth century. There is no doubt that the mouse and his child are on the same kind of quest for self-knowledge as Alice. In the *Wonderland* story, Alice evades the consequences of her dreams by waking; in the *Looking Glass* (its title betrays its psychological importance), Alice comes to terms with her dreams, her subconscious, and accepts her role as the White Queen. Since the mouse child sees and "knows himself" in the mirrored surface of the dog-food can, readers can expect some kind of self-acceptance, some kind of individuation for him in Hoban's story.

Although more adventures await the mouse and his child once they manage to escape from their muddy prison, they eventually find, albeit in a mouldering and decrepit condition, the dolls' house from the toy store where their story began. One by one they find the elephant and the rest of their friends from those halcyon days. In a rubbish dump, this motley group forms a family and learns the real meaning of life: to love one another. They make the dolls' house into a hotel for itinerant wind-up toys, bugs and small animals, and they call it—of course— "The Last Visible Dog." And the tramp who set the mouse and his child on the highway at the beginning of the story stumbles upon their establishment and pronounces a kind of blessing: "Be happy" (184). Hoban offers his young readers Paradise Regained, a kind of hope and a promise of real love, but it is very much a damaged and patched paradise. The ending is, I think, a sad one; the eking out of existence in a rubbish dump is hardly the stuff of which dreams are made. Nor is it a palliative to faltering faith. Nevertheless here there is a very clear articulation of hope; that existence is worth eking out if one can love and accept others, and be accepted oneself, in spite of missing limbs, clockwork which doesn't work, and the disfiguring effects of exposure and old age. And acceptance of self and of others is precisely the aim of the process of individuation.

Hoban's adult novel, *Riddley Walker*, draws from the same lexicon of puns and mysticism as that found in *The Mouse and his Child*, but as one might expect in a work aimed at a more sophisticated readership, there are some intellectual refinements. Nevertheless, what remains very clear is Hoban's debt to Lewis Carroll. The title of the novel, *Riddley Walker*, sets up a paradigm for the book's explorations of the great riddles of existence. Like the Alice books, Hoban's novel asks the unanswerable; not "why is a raven like a writing desk?", but "Why is Punch crookit? Why wil he all ways kil the babby if he can?" As with the riddle from Alice, the only response can be, "Parbly I wont never know it jus on me to think on it" (213).

There is much to "think on," however, in this text. The questions which are raised are part of human experience, and the choices laid before the character Riddley Walker are those available to us all. Part of the way in which Hoban uses his post-holocaust future to articulate hope, at least on an individual level, lies in his careful contrast between the spiritual death of the Waste Land, and the promise of the "Garden," the discovery of the Spirit of God. Hoban never uses these terms explicitly, but as I hope to show later in this chapter, they are certainly present by implication.

Despite what seems like traditional religious language, Hoban's fictional society is not Christian. It is a mystical blend of half-forgotten legends and stories of the saints, a superstitious following of seers and soothsayers, and an ancient nature-religion based upon a Moon Goddess. But, in syncretising this mixture of religious elements, Hoban succeeds in establishing some grounds for hope and some reasons for living, at least on a individual basis. And in doing so it seems that there is a certain distinguishing feature which Hoban implicitly attributes to fantasy: it concentrates upon the development of the individual rather than with global issues. While science fiction generally posits the notion of "saving the world" in one sense or another, fantasy is much more concerned with the spiritual and psychological growth of the individual. This distinction could account for the fact that there are on the market post-modernist science fiction texts such as Thomas Pynchon's *Gravity's Rainbow*, while fantasy is closer to Romanticism. It concentrates on the generation of meaning and rewards the hermeneutic approach. The invitation to hermeneutics is apparent even in such didactic recent works of fantasy as Martin Hocke's *The Ancient Solitary Reign* and Jeanette Winterson's surrealist *Sexing the Cherry*, both of which have a strong environmental message. But as both these authors show, the mere medium of the fantastic is not the message; it requires also the growth and development in some way or another of key characters to make the tale of fantasy work.

It is not surprising to find, then, that *Riddley Walker* is a *Bildungsroman*, more concerned about the spiritual rebirth of the main character than with "saving the world." In fact the world does not get "saved" at all.

The plot of the novel is very straightforward. It simply involves the efforts of a group of mutated humans (living in Kent almost two thousand years after a nuclear war) to re-invent technology, in particular gunpowder and the atomic bomb. The necessary ingredients are found and exploded, and the way seems clear to resuming the cycle of destruction which has brought humanity to this dismaying state.

Hoban's picture of post-holocaust humanity is sardonic. What comedy there is in the perverted myths and stories orally passed down through the generations is constantly subverted by tragedy. The human life-span has been considerably shortened, so that Riddley comes of age at twelve instead of twenty-one; the language has deteriorated into something resembling an extract from a very backward child's exercise book, and the reliance on superstition and stories also seems extremely childish. Perhaps there are resonances here of ancient wisdom: "Out of the mouths of babes and sucklings . . ." and the words of Christ, "Unless you become like little children, you shall not enter the Kingdom of Heaven" (Matt. 18:3). For Hoban, or at least for Riddley, "entering" the Kingdom is to learn first of all *where* the kingdom is, to locate it inside one's own being.

The critical reception to this book has not always been kind. Stephen Prickett finds the journey undertaken by Riddley to be almost impossible, given the amount of time allotted to it. Prickett believes that the journey was constructed by reference to maps, rather than from an intrinsic familiarity to the countryside.[1] This criticism is a valid one. When one considers the importance of "place" in fantasy, one must consider the necessity to "suspend disbelief." If the spirit of place is not credible, the credibility of the text is called into question and belief is not so much suspended as (to use Tolkien's acerbic comment made in another context),[2] hung, drawn and quartered. But if Hoban's distances have been incorrectly calculated, that cavil is surely only available to readers very familiar with the Kentish terrain. The spirit of the Waste Land of a post-holocaust England is very well evoked by the innocence of Riddley's first-person narrative and by the linguistic devices Hoban offers us.

We are not told until the beginning of Chapter 2 what the nature of this book is, although the title is rather more than suggestive of the operative metaphor. The opening lines of the second chapter, however, make the parameters of Riddley's story very clear:

> Walker is my name and I am the same. Riddley Walker. Walking my riddels where ever theyve took me and walking them now on this paper the same. (8)

Riddley, then, is a kinsman of C.S. Lewis's character Ransom in *Out of the Silent Planet*. Ransom is a Pedestrian, a word used in a punning sense since Ransom is also an unprepossessing kind of chap; a pedestrian sort of person, in fact. Ransom is the character Lewis uses for the reader to focus on and identify with as the story moves from the fields of cabbages and turnips to the colorful fantasia of the Martian landscape. Similarly, Frodo the hobbit, in Tolkien's *The Lord of the Rings*, is a pedestrian, walking his fearful burden to the Crack of Doom. These characters are "little men" (all are male); indeed there is something not a little hobbit-like in Riddley Walker. Having a character of this kind with which readers can identify is a highly polemic device; much can be communicated through the experiences of the character which will appeal very strongly to readers' emotions—in a literary exercise of a highly persuasive, intensely subversive kind.

Already in the first chapter, many questions have been raised, not the least by the inclusion of the myth of the "Hart of the Wud." This seems to be an account of a family fleeing from a town devastated by a nuclear blast, so infected with evil that the parents cannibalise their child and are themselves burned to death. In this myth also there appears the "clevver bloak," the figure symbolising technology and science, who prophesizes a return to an age of technology:

> 'Clevverness is gone now but littl by littl itwl come back. The iron will come back agen 1 day and when the iron comes back they wil bern chard coal in the hart of the wood.' (4)

This prophecy is fulfilled by the end of the book, with the discovery of gunpowder and the first explosion which heralds the return to an age of technology. There seems to be an element of inevitability about the redevelopment of technology which is highly pessimistic. Certainly in some of the more gruesome episodes in the book it seems that, despite two thousand years of suffering, deprivation and mutation, the human race has not changed a great deal.

Although the character Riddley is a "little man" or an Everyman, in his own society he is somewhat special. He is something of a seer, a "Connexion Man," who can interpret the utterances of the players in the travelling shows one of which reenacts the Eusa story. This is almost a priestly role in his futurist society; and as his spiritual development progresses, his priestly role changes; he becomes more explicitly a metonym for the artist and the author; his role is symbolic of *their* prophetic and priestly functions. Despite the obvious pessimism Hoban's plot offers for the long-term future of the world, all will be well, we may conclude, as long as there are prophets and priests of art and literature to mediate the spiritual aspects of existence to us.

The first intimation of Riddley's role as a connexion man comes at the end of Chapter 1, when Lorna, the tel woman, or tribal witch, explains that there is a force within each person which has no name, but which acts upon impulse and intuition. It is a spiritual force which "puts on us like we put on our cloes." That it is a spiritual force is quite clear from Lorna's rudimentary description of it:

'We aint a naturel part of it. We dint begin when it begun we dint begin *where* it begun. It ben here befor us nor I don't know what we are to it. May be weare jus only sickness and a feaver to it... It thinks us but it dont think *like* us...'

This strange inner force is never manifest tangibly ("beartht"), but it is present in nature, "in the woom of things its all ways on the road." Riddley, striving to grasp what the tel woman has told him, asks if this is a "tel" or prophecy for him. Her reply confirms his spiritual insight and destiny: "Riddley there aint nothing what *aint* a tel for you" (7). From that point on, the narrative follows Riddley's journeyings towards Canterbury Cathedral, in his time as in this the spiritual heart of the world in which he lives.

The essential plot then revolves about Riddley's great moral choice. He may join those who see to develop a new technology, or he may become an author/artist. It is clear that in this book technology is, if not an evil, then at the very least a corrupting force. As with other aspects of life in Riddley's post-holocaust world, the story of the corruption of the world by technology is encoded in myth. *The Eusa Story* is the primary myth of Riddley's culture, based upon a corruption of the Legend of St. Eustace found in Canterbury Cathedral, and made complex by the oral history which has combined the religious myth with stories of holocaust. The Eusa Story tells how the twentieth century world was wracked by wars until a final, major conflict arose. Eusa, a man who had turned from nature to the service of technology ("Mr Clevver") comments that "in norder to defent" themselves they will need "boats that go on the water & boats that go in the ayr & wewl need Berstin Fyr" (28). Mr Clevver suggests a quicker and easier way to end the war: "Thayr ar tu menne agenst us this tym we mus du betteren that. We keap fytin aul thees Warrs wy doan we jus du 1 Big 1... Yu mus fyn the Littl Shynin Man the Addom he runs in the wud" (29).

As the legend progresses, Eusa finds the Littl Man the Addom on the head of a stag, with his arms outstretched between the two antlers. Eusa pulls the little man in two ("splitting the atom"), and with the splitting of the atom two great dogs stand erect and begin to prophesy. As in *The Mouse and His Child*, the dogs have spiritual and prophetic significance, based upon the God/dog anagram. (Dogs also guide Riddley to Canterbury, a further indication of their roles as guardians and prophets.) But Eusa kills the dogs, and with the exploding of the atom, nature is devastated. Eusa tries to flee, but he is overcome and falls to the ground by a river, where the Littl Shynin Man appears to him and tells him that to be made whole, to restore the world, Eusa must go through the "Master Chayngis," "as menne as reqwyred... by the idear of yu" (34). The master changes referred to is a cycle of some kind (based apparently on the cycle of change-ringing the church bells), while it seems that "the idear" of a person is perhaps their spiritual identity, or the achievement of spiritual individuation. For Hoban, at least in the context of this novel, the "fall" of humanity is inextricably bound up with the unleashing of nuclear energy. The 1 Big 1 in the Eusa myth would seem to be the bombs which devastated Hiroshima and Nagasaki in World War Two, creating the most terrible and terrifying "Waste Land" that the world has ever known, a Waste Land which has undeniably spiritual signification given the contest of Power which has motivated the development of nuclear weaponry. And of course, it has been through a later and more sophisticated nuclear conflict that Riddley's home of Inland has been laid waste for two thousand years.

Like many other fantasy texts which take up the issue of Power, Hoban's novel expresses in graphically imaginative fiction Lord Acton's famous aphorism: "Power tends to corrupt, and absolute power corrupts absolutely. Great men are very often bad men" (504). While Hoban's novel is not immediately concerned with the issues of totalitarianism, it is very much concerned with the notion of exerting power over nature through technology, expressing something of the global angst of the present age and the omnipresent fear, mitigated slightly by the collapse of communism in Europe and by changing attitudes in the United States of America, of nuclear war. As Thomas J. Morrissey points out, the use of Canterbury as the focus for the idea of "Power" which Hoban develops in the novel is deeply significant:

> ...Cambry is the dead archetype of our civilization. Once a commercial center and seat of the English church, it was incinerated by the 1 Big 1 and is now surrounded by the Barrens, a sterile crescent left by the radiation. This place embodies the paradox that Riddley must grasp: how are man's intellectual and spiritual accomplishments compatible with his penchant for self-destruction? (211)

This raises for Riddley the issue of personal choice—whether to be associated with Power or whether to find "oneness" with Nature. The choices presented to Riddley are based partly on Gnosticism, partly on Taoism; on, as David Lake points out,

> the perennial philosophy of the Upanishads, Lao Tzu, Plotinus, Eckhart, Wordsworth, William Blake—and the Gnostic Gospel of Thomas, which furnishes the epigraph of this novel. (165)

The splitting of the Atom, and technology generally, is "twoness" or dividedness; while unity with Nature is wholeness or oneness. The dichotomy between the two, in which is encapsulated the issue of personal choice, is symbolised by Hoban's idiosyncratic use of Arabic figures in his text: 12 for twelve, 1 Big 1, and so on. David Lake adds that in the English language as in no other European language, there is confusion between 1 and I, a confusion exploited fully by Hoban (168). The dichotomies are carried further in juxtaposing the images of the "Waste Land" which is the legacy of technology and twoness, and the "Garden" which is the result of unity and wholeness. Indeed these dichotomies might be represented schematically:

Waste Land	Garden
(2000 + years after holocaust)	(Prehistory, mythic past rebirth of arts)
Burned Out Earth	Fertility
Technology	Nature
'Power' (science)	'Being' (mysticism)
Bernt Arse	Cambry
Yellerstone	Punch and Pooty
Twoness	Oneness
Atomic Fission	Entire Atom
Drop John, Aunty, Arga Warga	Not Struggling
(Struggling)	

In establishing these choices for Riddley, Hoban uses the futurist language which on first glance seems very simple, but which on closer acquaintance reveals an interplay of puns, multiple entendres, allusion, metaphors and metonomies. For example, "Eusa" is quite clearly a corruption of St. Eustace, but in the text it also carries the meaning of the political and technological imperialism of the USA (the nation which developed nuclear power, and which also has bases on British soil), and "User," since computer jargon occurs throughout the book. The language in which the story is narrated seems also to be a "Waste Land," but its fertility and wit require careful decoding.

The left hand column of the diagram above shows twoness, technology, death and disease (represented by the two devouring women "Aunty" and "Arga Warga," images of the devouring Anima of Jungian psychology, archetypes which recur in literature, and which are expressions of the male terror of the Vagina Dentata of ancient mythology). "Drop John" is a figure of human guilt or original sin, the burden humans carry for consenting to and participating in the destruction of Nature.

Opposed to these images of the Waste Land are the spiritual qualities which inform the creative impulse in the human being. We must create, not destroy; art, stories, and poetry, and therefore language, make us one with the creative forces in nature. The Goddess is also a female figure, the light Anima of Jung, the Earth Mother of ancient mythology. She is the Womb, the nurturer and the healer, the enveloping Oneness of Nature. When Riddley sees the ruins of the chancel of Canterbury Cathedral, he recognises in them the shape of the Goddess:

and in the still-standing pillars he sees images of forests, which are for lovers of Nature the true places of worship. But humans will always be faced with choices between Oneness and Twoness, the Waste Land and the Garden, which remain in opposition rather like the Yang and Yin of the Chinese Tao. (Morrissey, loc. cit.)

Perhaps one of the greatest achievements of this novel is the futurist language which Hoban uses. David Lake has written cogently on the way in which the language enables the complex series of puns and metaphors to be expressed with wit and economy (Lake, *passim*).[3] The language also embodies the mysticism of the novel, so that the "Littl Shynin Man the Addom" represents the *atom*, the mythical first man *Adam* and an American expression for aggressive behaviour, "up and *at them* (addem)." Since the riddles which give the book's protagonist his name are embodied in the language, Hoban becomes in this context at least, a modern Humpty Dumpty, making words mean what he wants them to mean; although he makes them mean more rather than less.

The future of humanity, as predicated in this novel, is fairly bleak— an endless cycle of technological Power-lust and of destruction. But Hoban articulates hope here, too; hope which depends upon individual human choices between the creation of a Waste Land or of a Garden. Through Riddley's choices, Hoban argues for a rebirth of spirituality in its widest sense—not of some absolutist and dogmatic religion, but of harmony with Nature, a questing, questioning spirituality which is expressed through creativity, through the priest-author who mediates to readers, or to those who hear the words spoken aloud, the riddles of the universe, and of the place of humanity within it. Riddley cannot offer answers, but "its jus on me to think on it." Riddley finds personal contentment and wholeness, despite the troubles of the world about him:

> Riddley Walkers ben to show
> Riddley Walkers on the go
> Dont go Riddley Walkers track
> Drop Johns ryding on his back.
>
> Still, I wunt have no other track. (213)

This ending clearly articulates hope. Like Alice, Riddley finds himself "crowned" with self-knowledge and maturity, contented from having made the right "moves" or choices for himself, yet aware that in the world about him disharmony will continue because of the destructiveness of technological power. The text is highly persuasive, arguing cogently for the recognition of the priestly role of the author. But all the devices Hoban uses serve also to urge readers to make right choices for themselves. And even if the novel fails to influence the readers' choices, there remains the hope that it will at least make us aware that we have them.

Chapter Seven
That Hideous 1984: Two Views on Dystopia[1]

Man is the only [animal] to whom the torture and
death of his own creatures is amusing in itself.
James Anthony Froude, *Oceana*

Much has been written in the past few decades of the way in which the mass media uses language. In particular, British linguist Paul Chilton takes issue with "Nukespeak," the language of the Cold War, which provides (he believes) examples of "interested manipulation of language" (54). Even the term "cold war" is a collocation of words which describe a war that was not really a war in the traditional sense, while simultaneously, "the word 'peace' has had its meaning changed (you might say perverted)" (49). What happens, according to Chilton, is that the producers of the "nukespeak" vocabulary do not communicate directly with the consumers; the language is "distributed" by the media, whose sources are Government departments and judiciously supplied "leaks" from official sources. The result is that the public have no avenue of response, and "are liable to regard what they see on television and read in the papers as objective and unbiased" (54). Chilton concedes, however, that the boundaries set out in his schematic representation of the processes of language production and the various roles of Government, the military, the media and the public are not "watertight...there are individuals who overstep them." Nevertheless, Chilton is concerned about the way the degradation of language is short-circuiting public responses, not only to nukespeak, but to other propagandist distortions of the language. George Orwell's Newspeak becomes highly relevant in the world of the mass media, especially since satellite communications often mean that events are covered for their "instant appeal" without any research or background being supplied. Such "instant" coverage is very much the province of television news, and it is becoming increasingly apparent that television news is the main source of information for many people.

Such a concern for language is not new. Chilton cites Jonathan Swift's *Voyage to Laputa* in which language is supposedly being 'improved and mechanised' by a technocratic elite:

The first Project was to shorten Discourse by cutting Polysyllables into one, and leaving out Verbs and Participles; because in Reality all things imaginable are but Nouns.

The other was a scheme for abolishing all Words whatsoever. And this was urged as a great Advantage in Point of Health as well as Brevity. For it is plain, that every word we speak is in some degree a Diminution of our Lungs by Corrosion; and consequently contributes to the shortening of our lives...(Swift, *Gulliver's Travels* 197-198, cited as *Voyage to Laputa* Ch 5 in Chilton 7)

So specific do these nouns become that it is argued that people should simply carry around the things about which they want to communicate, and save the bother of referring to them by means of words. However, the "Women in Conjunction with the Vulgar and Illiterate" object to this, and demand the right to speak with their mouths; but of course, as Swift notes with biting satire, this only goes to show what bitter enemies to Science such dissidents are. Chilton goes on to note that George Orwell's own polemical articles "Politics and the English Language" and "Politics vs. Literature," and his equally polemical novel, *Nineteen Eighty-Four*, owe much to Swiftian influences upon him (Chilton 6-7).

Interestingly, although Orwell objected to some aspects of Swift's world view, he continued to enjoy Swift's writings. Ironically enough, the particular emphases in Swift's work which Orwell most disliked appear in Orwell's own final novel. In particular, Orwell complains that

Swift falsifies his picture of the world by refusing to see anything in human life except dirt, folly and wickedness, but the part which he abstracts from the whole does exist, and it is something which we all know about while shrinking from mentioning it. Part of our minds—in any normal person it is the dominant part—believes that man is a noble animal and life is worth living: but there is also a sort of inner self which at least intermittently stands aghast at the horror of existence. ("Politics vs. Literature" 140)

This passage is preceded by Orwell's observation that"Swift is a diseased writer. He remains permanently in a depressed mood...." Similarly, Stansky and Abrahams write of the later Orwell that some of his early "bitterness and rancor" recur after the death of his wife, Eileen, "and reach a kind of concluding nightmarish intensity in *1984*" *(160)*.

The strong, perhaps even to some extent subconscious (if one is to accept Stansky and Abraham's above point) influence of Swift upon Orwell is significant when one turns to his contemporary, C.S. Lewis, who was addressing the same issues at almost the same time, and whose satirical prose (in *The Screwtape Letters*, and in certain episodes from his Ransom trilogy) exhibits a similar debt to Swift, since Orwell's work and Lewis's have much in common.

The notion of linguistic distortions, and the influence of the media, are featured in Lewis's novel *That Hideous Strength* which was published in 1945 and reviewed by Orwell in the *Manchester Evening News* of August 16 of that year. Orwell praised very highly some of the elements of Lewis's novel, but scorned Lewis's idea of supernatural intervention in the affairs of a totalitarian state. Orwell wrote: "[Mr. Lewis] is entitled to his beliefs, but they weaken his story, not only because they offend the average reader's sense of probability but because in effect they decide the issue in advance" (*Manchester Evening News* 2). This cavil apart, Orwell praised Lewis's other polemical points as being "all too topical in the light of the [at that time] all too recent atomic bombing of Japan." Orwell might have applied his comments to his own later work:

plenty of people in our age do entertain the monstrous dreams of power that Mr Lewis attributes to his characters, and we are within sight of the time when such dreams will be realisable. (*Loc cit*)

It is clear that at that time Orwell was pondering for himself the implication of uncircumscribed political power were it to be unleashed in his own country. His *Animal Farm* was released in the same year as *That Hideous Strength*, and it is worth noting the coincidence which has both Lewis and Orwell attacking a corrupt system in works ironically subtitled "A Fairy Story."

Orwell appropriates many of the same ideas that Lewis uses in *That Hideous Strength*, partly, I believe, because of the influence of Lewis's book, but also because the ideas had wide currency at that time. Indeed, Lewis had addressed them in 1943 in his Riddell Lectures at Durham University, later to be published as *The Abolition of Man*. As the title of the book suggests, Lewis believed that truncating the language and in particular emotive language, would create "men without chests," human beings with highly developed intellects, and quite lively bodily appetites, but without compassion, sympathy and those other human emotions which militate against mere intellectual cruelty. Lewis's warning is summarised in the final chapter of the essay which bears the same title as the book:

...The process which, if not checked, will abolish Man goes on apace among Communists and Democrats no less than among Fascists. The methods may (at first) differ in brutality. But many a mild-eyed scientist in *pince-nez*, many a popular dramatist, many an amateur philosopher in our midst, means in the long run just the same as the Nazi rulers of Germany. Traditional values are to be "debunked" and mankind to be cut out into some fresh shape at the will (which must, by hypothesis, be an arbitrary will) of some few lucky people in one lucky generation which has learned how to do it. The belief that we can invent "ideologies" at pleasure, and the consequent treatment of mankind as mere...specimens, preparations, begins to affect our very language. Once we killed bad men: now we liquidate unsocial elements. Virtue has become *integration* and diligence *dynamism* . . .

(Lewis, *Abolition* 44-45)

The novel *That Hideous Strength* takes up the cause, and uses fiction to show how "men without chests" might create a totalitarian society. In essence Orwell's novel repeats the same exercise.

It is useful to discuss Orwell's novel in comparison with Lewis's, since it would appear that the latter offers a hopeful, almost a traditionally happy, ending, while the former is uncompromisingly bitter, pessimistic and grim. Indeed it almost seems that looking for the articulation of hope in *Nineteen Eighty-Four* is a foolish and unrewarding endeavour. Nevertheless, hope can be found.

But in providing readers with hope both Lewis and Orwell sound a warning about the manipulative power of the media, a warning which has as much application to the present as it had in the 1940s, when Lewis and Orwell wrote. For example, in 1990, on April 25, the day Australians and New Zealanders celebrate "Anzac Day" commemorating their war dead and the servicemen and women of various theatres of war, a leading article appeared the "Anzac Day Supplement" of *The Courier-Mail*, the major daily newspaper in Queensland. Written by an associate editor of the paper, Peter Charlton, the article takes up the application by recent Australian historians of the words "myth" and "legend" to the gallant fight undertaken by Australian and New Zealand troops and Gallipoli in 1915. Militarily a disaster, the campaign nevertheless has become enshrined in Australian (and New Zealand) national history as a benchmark or rite of passage by which the new Commonwealth came of age. Charlton, himself a military historian, does not believe that this is the stuff of "legend" or "myth"; these words suggest an element of untruth about what is an historical fact. "Accuracy, at least in the choice of words, should be taken for granted in historians," Charlton laments (17).

The irony of Charlton's grievance lies in the fact that it is the *media* (of which he is an influential part) who introduce such terms because of the quality of larger-that-life heroism they give to certain events, and the way that those events have shaped cultural consciousness. For example, it is not uncommon for the media to refer to footballers as "legendary"; and very many sportsmen are also dubbed "heroes": surely this is cultural myth in the making. This is not to suggest that either Charlton or the media at large are "wrong" (the validity of either point could be argued at great length); merely to highlight the fact that even members of the media are aware of the distortions and manipulations of which it is capable. Charlton's linguistic and semantic point has been taken up also by Colin Bowles, writing for *The Australian*, which as its name suggests is the sole national daily newspaper in Australia. In fact Bowles shamelessly titles his article "Newspeak" and sighs, "Language is supposed to convey ideas and information as accurately as possible. But that fancy notion no longer holds true. In fact, it's quite the reverse" (43). He goes on to "translate" officialese and gobbledygook into "plain English." What both Bowles and Charlton utter is Wordsworthian theory, their ideal being "the real language of men [and women]" (Wordsworth 261). It is this same ideal, essentially Romantic, which both Lewis (an avowed neo-Romanticist) and Orwell (who would probably shudder at the appellation) pursue.

Where Hoban paints a grim picture of a cycle of technological invention and destruction, Lewis and Orwell suggest a more dangerous, because a more insidious, evil: a corruption that can grow, cancer-like, undetected, until power has been completely yielded to a circle of the political elite. What makes for interesting comparison, however, is the way in which all three books image the corruption and evil of a political and technological system through distortions of language, although Hoban's altered English actually enhances and enriches meaning though paronomasia, while Orwell and Lewis depict truncated meanings, or jargon without any meaning at all.

Despite some obvious correspondences between *Nineteen Eighty-Four* and *That Hideous Strength*, critics do not seem to have taken much account of them, except to draw attention to the debts both Orwell and Lewis owe to Chesterton (Steinhoff 17, Druker 26-64, Green and Hooper 102, 108, Gilfedder 5, Walzcuk 17-28). Nevertheless, these shared debts to such powerful polemicists as Swift and Chesterton obviously account for those points of view which Orwell and Lewis had in common. To begin with, they both chose the fantastic mode for their polemical novels. The subtitle to *That Hideous Strength* is "A Modern Fairy Story for Grown Ups" in order to justify the introduction of the supernatural and of Arthurian magic and polemic elements. Orwell's novel, on the other hand, is often regarded as science fiction. But the only "scientific advance" in the book is the two-way television network which allows constant surveillance. Otherwise, the novel seems to be all dreary realism and pessimism. Its setting with its "smell of boiled cabbage and old rag mats" is, however, almost surreal; it is an ugly world, but it is a fantasy world nevertheless, the diametrical opposite to "Wonderland" or William Morris's "Nowhere." Aspects of the real world have been altered to accommodate the rather abject character Winston Smith, who "was thirty-nine and had a varicose ulcer above his right ankle" (5). It is unusual for a man of that age to have a varicose ulcer; this is a world not unlike Riddley Walker's future Inland where human life spans have been contracted. It would seem, though, that the varicose ulcer, in the context of all the other gruesome imagery, serves a symbolic purpose. Humanity, symbolised by "the last man," is rotting away.

By the time Orwell comes to write about the evil of unrestrained political power in *Nineteen Eighty-Four*, he was very pessimistic about political systems. As Stansky and Abrahams point out, "at the heart of Orwell's socialism...was a belief in honour and decency," and his experiences in the Spanish Civil War disabused him of the notion that for others, the same ethics held true (229). So it is not surprising to find something of the same bitterness in the torture chamber scenes in Room 101 which represent the deception and unmitigated evil of Big Brother's regime. Winston, rather naively, tries to rationalise the power structure and its cruel imposition of mindless conformity upon its victims. "'You are ruling us for our own good'," he offers. But O'Brien, whose real identity we never know (the Head of the Thought Police? Big Brother himself?) replies, "'We are not interested in the good of others: we are interested solely in power...only power, pure power...The object of torture is torture, the object of power is power'" (211-212). In other words, the assumption and retention of power is an end in itself, not a means to an end. And torture, brainwashing and dehumanisation are essential to the maintenance of a regime intoxicated by and addicted to power itself. Thus all human values, even the "spirit of man," must be eradicated so that a few—O'Brien among them—may profit by the subjection and the humiliation of many. There is no doubt that O'Brien profits from his participation in Big Brother's atrocities: "'We...have privilege'," he admits. He serves wine while Winston and his fellow citizens are issued with cheap gin, and upon O'Brien's desk is "a silver box of cigarettes...very good cigarettes" (141).

As the opening paragraphs of the novel suggest, this is a book about betrayal; April is the month in which Easter most often occurs, and with it Good Friday, the commemoration of a betrayal. The clocks are striking thirteen, not particularly unusual if a twenty-four hour clock is used; but thirteen is also the number of betrayal and bad luck. The bleakest moments of the book occur when it becomes clear that Winston is betraying himself, and all humanity. Like Riddley Walker, like Frodo the Hobbit, Winston is a "common man" (his surname is *Smith*, the commonest surname in English). But his first name, obviously some kind of reference to Winston Churchill, suggests at least the possibility of greatness. Unfortunately the suggested promise of the name is undermined, and this character is no hero. There is something amiss in him all along, which the reader can only witness with dismay as time and again Winston entraps himself through self-deception.

In contrast with Orwell's humanist values, the values which Lewis sets up in his novel are spiritual ones. Behind the devilry in his Waste Land of technology at Belbury lurks real devilish power in the form of "Macrobes" who are invoked by the elite of the National Institute for Co-ordinated Experiments, an exceedingly nasty institution served by the ironic acronym "N.I.C.E." But of course, as with Orwell's glass paperweight, the elegant diary, and the cosy love-nest above Mr. Charrington's store, this is a world where "fair is foul and foul is fair." Mark Studdock, the rather gormless husband of the book's leading female character, is seduced by the promise of power at Belbury, being driven there by Lord Feverstone who is "a big man driving a big car to somewhere where they would find big stuff going on" (Lewis 56). The final test of Mark's readiness for full initiation into the grisly mysteries of Belbury takes place in the Objective Room, which has a very similar purpose to that of Orwell's Room 101: to kill all specifically human reactions in him so that he would willingly participate in the obscenities of the occultic, technologically and scientifically insane machinations of the N.I.C.E. (369).

The plan goes wrong. Mark's experiences in the Objective Room, where all architecture, furnishings and artwork are vaguely and almost subliminally obscene, serves only to awaken in him the desire for "something he vaguely called 'the Normal'" (370). This human value is not far removed from that which for Orwell provided the basis for human and objective values, "common decency." It is "common decency" which Winston Smith loses when he screams, in the closing chapters of *Nineteen Eighty-four*, "Do it to Julia!... Not me! I don't care what you do to her. Tear her face off, strip her to the bones. Not me! Julia! Not me!" (230). This passage is tragic, not so much for the way Winston betrays his lover, but for the way in which he betrays the humanity in himself.

In both novels, the ruling technocracies are anxious to outlaw sexual intercourse. At Belbury, one of the primary aims of the N.I.C.E. is to subdue nature and all things organic. The Waste Land created there is both spiritual and, in every sense of the word, physical: "There will never be peace and order and discipline so long as there is sex" (211). Of course sex to Lewis is part of the divine order, and necessarily means the subjection of the female to the male—Jane Studdock's fate in the "happy" ending. Orwell follows Lewis by having Big Brother regulate the biological functions of his victims by eradicating the sexual act, which "successfully performed, was rebellion" (58). Instead of human desire and arousal, "all children had to be begotten by artificial insemination (*artsem* as it was called in Newspeak) and brought up in public institutions" (56). Like Aldous Huxley, Orwell and Lewis saw biology and psychology as the scientific loci for the dehumanising process of a totalitarian regime (Huxley, *Letters* 534).

Possibly the most sinister aspect of both novels, and where they are closest, is in their shared motif of the corrupted or perverted logos. It is in this respect, too, that the concerns of the two novels are most closely relevant to the current political and social *Zeitgeist*. In Orwell's novel, the motif is of course known as "Newspeak," which has become over the last generation or so a term applicable to almost any perceived corruption of language. But in the novel, Newspeak is a carefully crafted linguistic device imposed in stages upon an unprotesting (because powerless) public. Orwell's appendix to *Nineteen Eighty-Four* clearly defines the purpose of the new language: "to provide a medium of expression for the world-view and mental habits proper to the devotees of Ingsoc, [and] to make all other modes of thought impossible" (241). Words are denuded of connotative or associative meanings, the vocabulary is systematically reduced, portmanteau words extend meanings, but only within severely circumscribed limits, and acronyms add to the jargon which Orwell thought was the foundation of corrupt political language. If language is the human mechanism for conceptualising, then any repression or inhibition imposed on language necessary limits the ability to conceptualise. Language couched in jargonistic terms reveals, Orwell writes, that "the writer either has a meaning and cannot express it...or he is almost indifferent as to whether his words mean anything or not." He goes further. "Political language...is designed to make lies sound truthful and murder respectable, and to give an appearance of solidity to pure wind" (Orwell, "Politics and the English Language" 145, 157).

In the Newspeak appendix, Orwell coins the term "Duckspeak"— "to quack like a duck"—to illustrate the respective meaninglessness and deception of Newspeak and Big Brother's society, since "Duckspeak" does not require the concomitant operation of intellect and voice box; "a Party member called upon to make a political judgement should be able to spray forth automatically as a machine gun spraying forth bullets" (248). But even in the main text of the book, where Newspeak is only used to exemplify aspects of it, language is maneuvered to subvert any possible hope which might be available in the narrative. For example, there seems to be some kind of metaphysical promise in O'Brien's prophecy that Winston should meet him "in the place where there is no darkness" (145); but to O'Brien the words are no more than Duckspeak. For him there is no metaphysical meaning; he refers, as Winston later discovers, to Room 101.

Although Lewis attached a similar importance to language, his Christian beliefs impelled him to see language as an imitation of the Divine Logos, the Word of God made flesh. His villains speak jargon because they are evil ("out of the mouth the heart speaks" [Matthew 15:18]); thus the spectral Wither, Deputy Director of the N.I.C.E., never utters a meaningful sentence, although this fact is somewhat disguised by his circumlocutions. In response to Mark Studdock's direct inquiry about the exact nature of his work, Wither tells him: "There has never been the least question of that sort. It has always been understood that your co-operation with the institute would be entirely acceptable—would be of the highest value" (125). This is hardly a definite answer. Again, at the banquet in the concluding chapters of the novel, the dysphasia of which Jules is the first victim initially goes unnoticed. Wither, master of unmeaning, is the last to detect it. Paul Chilton observes that "the quasi-mystical theme of the ideal and universal language," and that theories of language reflecting "philosophical, ethical and political concerns" are linked with the Biblical account of the tower of Babel, especially in science fiction (we might also add fantasy) (2). Chilton's reading in the genres is not very extensive: it overlooks Lewis's *That Hideous Strength*, the very title of which is taken from the lines included in the epigraph:

The Shadow of that hyddeous strength
Sax myle and more it is of length.

These lines are from the Sir David Lyndsay's *Ane Dialog*, a medieval text which describes the Tower of Babel, to which the name 'Belbury' alludes. The confusion of tongues in the banquet scene at Belbury is very clearly a re-interpretation of the Babel story. At St. Anne's, where in contrast with the Waste Land of Belbury, there is a prolific garden, and where a remnant of people loyal to Christianity, or at least to Christian values, remains, there is a visitation of Mercury, the Lord of Meaning, who imbues the normally logical and referential language used there with "toppling structures of double meaning, . . . sky rockets of metaphor and allusion" (397-98).

Both Lewis and Orwell extend their account of the perverted logos into the public arena *per medium* of the news which provides the majority of a nation's citizens with their only insights into political affairs. It is here that the two novels impinge most upon current cultural concerns, here too, that both authors exhibit deep scepticism. In *That Hideous Strength*, Mark Studdock, in the pay of the N.I.C.E., writes an account of a riot in Edgestow twenty-four hours before the event, after Feverstone jokes that "'You surely don't need to wait for a thing to happen before you tell the story of it'!" (158). The articles which Mark produces demonstrate Lewis's own gift of Swiftian satire: they are written in the respective styles of the intellectual and the sensational press. This is more than a trifle sinister when one bears in mind that although journalists like to maintain the fiction that news is unpredictable, relentlessly hunted down by daring and fearless reporters, the opposite is in fact true. Most news is predictable, and the daily diaries of events kept in most news organisations mean that coverage of events is planned well in advance (Golding and Elliott 97).

Winston Smith, in Orwell's novel, rewrites the news to comply with current propaganda. "In this way every prediction made by the Party could be shown by documentary evidence to have been correct; nor was any item of news, or any expression of opinion, which conflicted with the needs of the moment, ever allowed to remain on record" (35). The similarity of these accounts of manipulating the public mind suggests that the pessimism which pervades them might have had wider currency than merely each novelist's imagination.

Both these novels, with their bleak views of society, and with their dire predictions for the fate of the English language at the hands of politicians and scientists, are heavily sceptical and pessimistic. Lewis, a Christian, offers a "happy ending" through supernatural intervention. But one must accept the validity of Orwell's criticism of Lewis's gratuitous inclusion of the supernatural. And there is certainly some doubt about the "happiness" of the ending. Belbury is destroyed in a bloodbath of bestial rage, while Jane Studdock is overcome with romantic love and sexual arousal at the sight of her husband's shirt hanging out of the window of their house. She goes in to him, ready to submit herself to him, an ending calculated to raise the ire of not a few female readers in 1945, and many more in the 1990s. Still, Lewis offers hope; but the hope is based upon an almost hopeless ideal of Christian marriage and the cosmic or spiritual power associated with it. At the beginning of the book, Jane is lonely, left at home to clean, to rummage through the notes for her doctoral thesis on "Donne's triumphant vindication of the body" (10). At the end of the book, "normality" has been restored, but surely that bodes more loneliness, if submissively accepted, for an unhappy Jane?

The oppositions between the Waste Land and the Garden in Lewis's novel are straightforward and show quite clearly what seems to be a simple choice:

Waste Land	Garden
Belbury	St. Anne's
(Down in a valley)	(Up on a hill)
Sterility (organic life	Fertility
& sexuality abolished,	
Lesbianism)	
Winter Images	Summer/Autumn Images
cold, dark	warm, gold, light
Ambition	Obedience
Greed	Humility

Poised between these oppositions are Merlin the resurrected Arthurian magician, and Jane and Mark Studdock. Both the physical and the cosmic outcomes depend on the choices these three make.

By contrast, Orwell's rhetoric is essentially the rhetoric of pessimism. Nevertheless he too offers against his Waste Land a "garden" of warmth and fecundity denied to the citizens of Ingsoc. This is the realm of the proles:

> The June sun was still high in the sky, and in the sun-filled court below, a monstrous woman, solid as a Norman pillar, with brawny red forearms and a sacking apron strapped about her middle, was stumping to and fro between a washtub and a clothes line, pegging out a series of square white things which Winston recognised as babies' diapers. (113)

The world of the proles is primitive: "Proles and animals are free" according to the Party (61), but there is also a primeval force in the fecundity and sexual freedom allowed them. But the "garden" of the proles is related to the paradise of the Eloi in H. G. Well's *The Time Machine*—in that here, too, there is a very real sense of exploitation of the underprivileged. Although earthy and basic emotions and sexual fulfilment are allowed, intellect is repressed; whereas the Party forbids eroticism for its intellectuals and extols the virtues of Artsem. Winston suggests that "if there is hope, it lies in the proles," (69, 72) but Winston is an unreliable source and his other hopes are all cruelly dashed. But there are other intimations, albeit outside the text, of a "garden" which offers to readers if not to the characters certain choices. Schematically, the oppositions might be represented in the following way:

Waste Land	'Garden'
Ingsoc	Ideal Society
Technology	Nature
Artsem	Fecuncity
Big Brother	Individuality
Hatred	Love (eroticism)
Torture	Endurance
Lies	Truth
Slogans	Reason, Thought
Jargon	Poetry, Song
Spying (in families)	Trust, Freedom

Julia and Winston attempt, at least in part, to choose the "Garden," but for them it is too late. Nor do the proles have any real choice. The reader, however, has.

For Winston, the notion that there is a choice is simply one more hopeful idea which Orwell cruelly and bitterly subverts. Nowhere is this undermining or deconstructing of hope more dismaying than in the notion that one might die, but die with honour. After the secret meeting with O'Brien, Winston ruminates:

> . . . if the object was not to stay alive but to stay human, what difference did it ultimately make? They could not alter your feelings: for that matter you could not alter them yourself, even if you had wanted to. They could lay bare in the utmost detail everything that you had done or said or thought; but the inner heart, whose workings were mysterious even to yourself, remained impregnable. (136)

These brave thoughts are cruelly countered at the end of the book by the gin-sodden, rotting wreck of an inhuman being which Winston has become. His mind and his feelings have been appropriated by Big Brother: he has remained alive, but not human.

There is hardly any doubt about the scepticism in Orwell's novel; if every image of hope is ruthlessly subverted, it is surely difficult to detect in it the articulation of hope. It is, however, profoundly present, although it is subtextual rather than textual. The novel has become something of a catchword, part of the cultural mythology of the West, where those who have never turned its pages are nevertheless familiar with the concepts of "Newspeak" and "Big Brother." The feared imposts of totalitarianism in the aftermath of World War Two and the division of Europe have not occurred in stable Western democracies, and the English language, though growing and changing at a pace not appreciated by all its speakers, has never had imposed upon it the forceful circumscriptions of Newspeak. And while the language is growing and changing "naturally," as it were, one might take comfort that the warnings sounded by the ill and world-weary Orwell have been heeded. One needs only to take account of the articles and letters freely printed in the academic and in the popular press about political jargon and the perversions of the tongue to know that "someone" is watching the watchers, and that Big Brother has not yet assumed ultimate power. While Chilton is free to criticise the currency of the Newspeak vocabulary, and Charlton can publicly lament the misuse of certain terms by historians, there is till a measure of freedom. Such staunch defenders of the language maintain the prophetic tradition of Orwell and Lewis, and (though perhaps less obviously) of Wordsworth and Coleridge as well. And with that comes the hope—sometimes, as in the years of the Cold War, very faint, but in these times perhaps much brighter—that the pessimistic vision of *Nineteen Eighty-Four* may never come to pass. And that hope is surely the stronger for Orwell's bleak contribution to fantasy literature. Lewis's book touches on the same or similar themes, but it cannot be denied that it lacks the power and compulsion of Orwell's darker vision. In *Nineteen Eighty-Four*, Lord Acton's warning, "all power tends to corrupt, and absolute power corrupts absolutely" is fictionalised in a terrifying way. We have, I think, Orwell to thank that it remains, at least for the most part, in the realm of fiction and fantasy.

In setting out their dire warnings, both Lewis and Orwell fulfill the prophetic role of the author/priest. Lewis's text is "religious," Orwell's is sceptical. And yet both texts operate in essentially the same space. Lewis tries very hard to persuade his readers to have faith. I think perhaps he tries too hard, and ends by being didactic and unconvincing. But his mysticism and his cosmic vision certainly articulate hope, and in that, perhaps, as well as in the warnings he issues, lies the value of his book.

To refer to Orwell's subversive linguistic tactics as deconstructive writing would be anachronistic; in any case he is not a programmatic deconstructor. Nevertheless, his relentless undermining of hope in every instance when it is seemingly offered provides the dynamic of his novel. But he, like Lewis, is performing a prophetic function. His characters have no choice, but he evokes the notion of an ideal language lost in the historically occluded past. Largely thanks to his tragic polemic and the myths that it has generated about language and political power in the years since he wrote it, his readers—so far—still have the right and the freedom to make choices.

Chapter Eight
Religion and Romanticism in *The Neverending Story*

> ...*Romantic poetry works by means of symbols*
> *rather than analogies or allegories because it is*
> *concerned to change the way the reader experiences life.*

> Stephen Prickett, *Coleridge and Wordsworth:*
> *The Poetry of Growth*, 15

Michael Ende's intricate fantasy novel *The Neverending Story* is, according to the cover blurb, an international bestseller. But despite its translation from German into English and its access to the lucrative American market, and following that its adaptation into films of the same name, the novel has slipped quietly from critical notice. This oversight is lamentable, because the book has a great deal of value to offer not only to young readers at whom it was ostensibly aimed, but to adults as well. In particular, it offers some insights into the complex worlds of the imagination and of the human psyche, and addresses whether consciously or not some of the concerns of contemporary literary theory.

The Neverending Story is, above all, a profoundly religious text, although there is not a word in it that is specifically religious, and in it there are unmistakable elements of scepticism. But through this text, the author's priestly role can be seen quite clearly, and the problematics of fantasy are dealt with in a context which includes spiritual, as well as psychological growth. This is no mere fairy tale, though it invokes the whole fairy story tradition. It is a work of the Romantic Imagination, and its purpose is, as Stephen Prickett has noted in the epigraph to this chapter, "to change the way the reader experiences life" (15). In other words it offers a lived "dialectic of Desire" as Bastian Balthazar Bux pursues his ambitions and daydreams through the wonders of Fantastica, the world of fantasy and imagination. As C.S. Lewis has written in another context, "The dialectic of Desire, faithfully followed, would retrieve all mistakes, head you off from all false paths, and force you not to propound, but to live through, a sort of ontological proof." Lewis was writing of his own experiences of the strongly nostalgic emotion of *Sehnsucht,* the desire for something which can hardly be identified, but which

pierces us like a rapier at the smell of a bonfire, the sound of wild ducks flying overhead, the title of The Well at the World's end, the opening lines of *Kubla Khan,* the morning cobwebs in late summer, or the noise of falling waves...." (10)

This same longing is generated for Michael Ende's character Bastian by the experience of reading, indeed by the physical object of a book itself:

'I wonder,' he said to himself, 'what's in a book while its closed. Oh, I know it's full of letters printed on paper, but all the same, something must be happening, because as soon as I open it, there's a whole story with people I don't know yet and all kinds of adventures and deeds and battles. And sometimes there are storms at sea, or it takes you to strange cities and countries. All those things are somehow shut up in a book. Of course, you have to read it to find out. But it's already there, that's the funny thing. I just wish I knew how it could be.' (11)

There is in this passage an undoubted ontological impetus: a world has been created and is waiting for the reader to enter it. And as Tolkien has written in his essay "On Fairy Stories," the reader must enter and engage with this secondary world and with its special laws (Tolkien 48). But Ende's text is polysemous; there is a fantasy within a fantasy. There is the primary tale of the small boy Bastian with which the reader engages, and there is the story of Fantastica into which Bastian finds himself drawn. The self-reflexivity of the tale makes it highly meta-narratological. The alternation of red and green typeface (in the original versions, both German and English) also emphasizes the meta-narrative technique. This might be seen as an attempt to undermine the operation of the imaginative process, since there is a deliberate return to the fictional version of the "real" world and the notion of readerly engagement within a text.

But this, of course, is not the whole story. The role of Bastian in the metafictional world parallels the role of the reader in the act of reading any text. Readers must construct the text, as modern theorists would have it; the author is "dead" and meaning resides only in the subjective engagement of the reader with the signifying constructs which comprise the text. Certainly Bastian "constructs" the text; but the text in this novel is much more than merely words on paper, as Bastian is well aware. The text is a world, and reading the act of creating a world, which is precisely the role Bastian is given in the world of Fantastica. Moreover, he is constantly referred to as a "Savior" by the inhabitants of Fantastica, which emphasizes his creative and godlike function, although this *deus ex machina* from the mundane world is a flawed savior whose endeavors are not always either well-intentioned or beneficent in their effects.

This is, to a very great degree, a *Bildungsroman* in the style of Hoban's *Riddley Walker*, tracing as it does the moral and psychological development of one key character, from whose point of view the narrative is related. Though not told in the first person (indeed it *cannot* be told in the first person, since at one point Bastian loses his memory completely) there is no doubt about its focus. And like Riddley Walker and Frodo, like Jane and Mark Studdock and Winston Smith, Bastian is an "Everyperson," a very ordinary, unprepossessing, and decidedly unremarkable small boy, rather plump, and neither very selfless nor very courageous. His main claims to readerly sympathy arise from his sadness at his mother's death and the way he has been excluded from his father's affections by the parent's preoccupations with his own grief, and, of course, there is something appealing in Bastian's abiding love for books.

This sympathy is eroded a trifle in Bastian's act of removing the book from Mr. Coreander's shop in the opening episodes; but this is balanced almost immediately by the boy's remorse and by the way he later takes responsibility for his deed at the end of the book. It turns out that, after all, the book was "his story" and meant specially for him. These mitigating circumstances are not divulged until the end, because it is necessary that Bastian is not seen as an altogether likeable character at the beginning. All the errors he makes in Fantastica arise out of his own psyche, although he does not realize it; he must discover himself in order to make the right sort of wish, so that he can complete his dual quest. For not only must Bastian restore the world of the Imagination, but he must allow the Imagination to heal the real world.

In many respects, this novel has resonances of, and intertextual relationships with, the literature of Romanticism in its various manifestations. There are certainly some Coleridgean overtones, especially in the notion of perception and creativity. The world of Fantastica is one in which there can be no new creation; rather what happens is that elements of the Fantastican world are "dissolved, dissipated and diffused," and recombined into different forms. For true creativity to be manifested in Fantastica, human intervention is needed: Bastian's role as savior is that also of creator. When he returns to the real world, he comes also as a savior, bringing the Water of Life to his emotionally imprisoned father. And in giving his father the ability to see life afresh, and to experience joy and beauty once again, Bastian exercises his abilities to create and to heal. When the roles are transferred from the fantasy world to the real world, they are contracted from the universal to the particular, another point which may be seen as "religious": divine intervention, performed through individual humans, may affect either the whole world, or one individual only. In Bastian, through the operation of the Imagination, we have in the words of William Blake,"Eternity contracted to a span...Infinity in a grain of sand."

In the treatment of Infinity or of "neverendingness," there is a resemblance in this text to the *Alice* books and to Hoban's *The Mouse and His Child*. Here, however, Infinity can be contemplated by the endless retelling of the tale, which without input from the human imagination, is destined to be endlessly repeated, a "neverending story." A neverending story sounds like a great idea to the avid reader; the title of the book in Mr. Coreander's shop attracts Bastian, who always feels sad when he finishes reading a much-loved tale. But as with every other imaginative element in the novel, "neverendingness" can be both good and evil. And the neverendingness of the story before the coming of Bastian has about it the quality of despair, a kind of dull and onerous literary treadmill from which only the human imagination can provide escape.

There is an interesting treatment of the concepts of good and evil in this book. In Fantastica, the Childlike Empress regards good and evil characters alike. All are creations of the human imagination. As Tolkien writes in his poem "Mythopoeia:"

> Though all the crannies of the world we filled
> with Elves and Goblins, though we dared to build
> Gods and their houses out of dark and light,
> and sowed the seed of dragons—'twas our right
> (used or misused).
>
> (Tolkien 49)

The human imagination has access to both "dark and light"; in the worlds of fantasy there are good and evil characters who are equally important to the story. Quests would not appeal were there not monsters to be overcome and evil creatures to outwit; they are all part of the "story." In Fantastica, then, the evil characters are as valuable as the good ones, since they arise out of the same creative human faculty. Human Imagination is a dualistic faculty, and human creators are dualistic gods since they are, as Tolkien suggests in his poem, "lords in rags"—fallen creatures. Although Ende does not articulate this point explicitly, it is implicit in the value he places upon the evil characters in his fantastic world—a world which clearly comprises all the realms of human imagination: myth, fantasy, legend, story, parable, allegory and *Märchen*. The real evil in Fantastica, the terrifying threat to the world of the imagination, is "the Nothing," the sense of absence and loss which pervades the story until Bastian can "enter" the fictional realm. And it is the idea of "the Nothing" which comes closest in this novel to commentary upon recent theoretical trends in literature.

It is very difficult to describe the Nothing. It is, in this novel, utter absence—not pain, not loss, but mere absence. The word, as used in the context of Ende's novel, does not mean merely "unknowable" or "indescribable" as it sometimes does in literature for children. For example, in the very old Walt Disney cartoon, *Dumbo the Elephant,* a bat looks at the elephant's big ears and sings rather insultingly, "At least a bat is something/ A silly and a dumb thing/ But you're nothing but a nothing..." Dumbo, however, *is* something. Michael Ende's Nothing is nothing, as the will-o'-the-wisp tries to explain:

'Something has happened in Moldymoor...something impossible to understand. Actually, it's still happening. It's hard to describe—the way it began was—well, in the east of our country there's a lake—that is, there *was* a lake—Lake Foamingbroth we called it. Well, the way it began was like this. One day Lake Foamingbroth wasn't there anymore—it was gone. See?'

'You mean it dried up?' Gluckuk inquired.

'No,' said the will-o'-the-wisp. 'Then there'd be a dried-up lake. But there isn't. Where the lake used to be there's nothing—absolutely nothing. Now do you see?'

'A hole?' the rock chewer grunted.

'No, not a hole,' said the will-o'-the-wisp despairingly. 'A hole, after all, is something. This is nothing at all.' (19)

This notion of non-presence is very close to the Derridean concept of endless deferrals, by which contextual meaning can never be established because no contextual environment can ever supply the terminus of significance. In other words, for Derridean deconstructors, referential meaning is never achieved (Nuttall 24). Any notion of Presence only serves deconstructors for an emptiness which readers desire to fill; it is a "supplement," something added to rectify a lack or deficiency— a "nothing." Ultimately and essentially, "Derridean deconstruction consists of showing that the whole edifice of Western metaphysics rests on the possibility of compensating for a primordial nonpresence by way of supplement" (Harari 34). As A.D. Nuttall makes clear, what is involved in programmatic deconstruction of this kind is the dissolution of self, of experience and of meanings (36) which provide termini for literary symbols. Moreover, Nuttall points out, the text itself is seen to be

...henceforth no longer a finished corpus of writing, some constant enclosed in a book or its margins, but in a differential network, a fabric of traces referring endlessly to something other than itself, to other differential traces. (*loc.cit.*)

Is Michael Ende, constructing his neverending story, playing deconstructive games? Certainly, the story is circular until Bastian is drawn into the world of Fantastica. Once there, Bastian begins to deconstruct his own "self," since with every magic wish conferred on him by the magical amulet he loses part of his memory, and part of his own cognition of himself. But if this is deconstruction, it is not very convincing, since Ende rehabilitates Bastian and sends him back to the real world, where there is real hope for the future in Bastian's demonstration of maturity and wisdom, and in his father's realisation that there is, indeed, something to live for in caring for his son.

Ende effectively undermines the deconstructive impetus he so carefully builds into his novel, and it is very plain from the context of the "nothing" and its effect on the world of the Imagination that this text is counter-deconstructive. That is not to say that it is without elements of scepticism. They abound, but they, too, are part of the Imaginative world. There is no god in the world of Fantastica, but logically there cannot be. For the god of secondary worlds is a secondary god—that is, the author/creator. This is the Coleridgean notion of the Secondary Imagination at work, and Tolkien's extrapolation from Coleridgean theory of the notion of sub-creation. And as David Jasper has succinctly pointed out, Coleridge's theory of the Imagination is not merely a theory of aesthetics, but deeply theological:

> It is, however, through objects—whether palace domes, albatrosses or embers in the grate—in their symbolic role of particulars which enunciate the whole, that the imagination works by drawing upon the 'inward experience' of man made as a creative soul in God's image. (Jasper 79)

It is not surprising that echoes of Coleridge should be manifested in the work of a twentieth-century German fantasist, since Coleridge's own thinking was profoundly influenced by German thinkers such as Friedrich Schlegel and his brother, A.W. Schlegel, Novalis, Kant and Schelling (Jasper 8-19). And Jasper remarks in the context of his discussion of Coleridge that "The poet's task is a religious one. Poetic inspiration lays upon him the prophetic burden of mediating divine revelations to mankind" (19). This is precisely the calling of the writer of fantasy, the role of the priest/prophet who articulates hope to an increasingly despairing humankind, and in particular to those contemporary critics who accept the necessity for subversion and undermining certain elements of meaning within texts, but who seek deliverance from the all-devouring "nothing" of extremist nihilistic deconstruction. Ende, I believe, is one of the latter, at least as far as this novel is concerned.

The remedy for the encroaching Nothing is for a human to venture into Fantastica in order to give the Childlike Empress a new name. This element of the complex plot permits a limited discussion of the language of the novel. I have avoided commenting in detail upon the basic element of the book because I am using a translation. A scholar much more learned in German than I, with access to the original text, is obviously better qualified to discuss the linguistic aspects of this novel. But the

notion of naming is something that this book has in common with
Tolkien and Le Guin, where names not only embody identity (as with
the true names of the Ents and the mystical potency of true names in
Earthsea) but are also the sources of empowering, not only of the possessor
of the name, but also of those who know and use it.

The Childlike Empress is not, we are told, an ordinary inhabitant
of Fantastica. She is ageless, and although she bears the title "empress"
she does not exert any rule over her dominions. She symbolises, perhaps,
the realm of the subconscious mind, where archetypal images and shapes
are manifested and from which the Imagination springs. And naming
is surely an exercise of the imagination, even in such a pragmatic
endeavour as naming a child; for even in the mundane world names
have very strong connotative and associative meanings. In the English
school stories, which were so popular in this century up until the nineteen
sixties, the wicked female prefects were invariably called "Sybil," "Vera"
or "Gertrude;" the heroic Fourth Formers who saved the school rejoiced
in such names as "Pat," "Judy" or "Christine." The same device was
featured in boys' school stories, with the plotters having either foreign
names, or being called "Sylvester" or "Cyril," while the courageous lads
of the Lower Fourth had names such as "Michael," "Terry" and "David."
These names, even in pseudo-realistic school stories, were almost generic
in operation; once a character appeared with a name drawn from any
of these sets (my list is hardly exhaustive) there were set up immediately
for the reader generic expectations of some kind of moral attitude. Bastian
names the Childlike Empress "Moon Child," a name laden with
connotations of softness, light, gentleness and beauty. But a Moon Child
is a creature as much of shadow as light, so that the dualistic aspects
of Fantastica are embodied in the Empress.

In the two snakes which appear on the cover of Bastian's book,
and which make up the magical amulet "AURYN," the same duality
appears: one snake is black, the other white. Although the design is
rather different from the Taoist Yin/Yang symbol, the two snakes are
meant, I believe, to represent, at least to some extent, the same kind
of world view. After all, the good arises from the bad; from the
encroachment of the Nothing comes the new name for the Childlike
Empress; and Bastian's magic in Fantastica, though occasionally well-
intentioned, upsets a certain "balance" in the elements of the imaginary
world. Ende is rather more skillful at concealing the message than Le
Guin, whose *Earthsea* is highly didactic; Ende conveys something of
the same message, but it is not easy to detect what his own *Weltanschauung*
actually is. And perhaps that is why his fantasy is so compelling; but
it might also account for the fact that *The Neverending Story* has not
become a cultic work in the same way as *The Lord of the Rings* and
The Earthsea Trilogy. For although these two works can be perceived,

as this study shows, as highly sceptical works, they appear, at least superficially, to be offering certainties. Ende, on the other hand, seems to be offering uncertainties, at least in the context of the Fantastican world; and yet the hope he articulates lies in the operation of the Imagination—a faculty which is for him as for Coleridge, profoundly theological. Bastian's adventures in Fantastica demonstrate this point very well.

As Bastian wishes Fantastica back into being, his own personality diminishes and his memories of the "real" world fade. Bastian becomes arrogant and self-deluded, since he cannot be made aware of the fact that he has forgotten details of the past; for him, in the moment of forgetting, there never *was* a past. While Bastian's personality fades, however, the personalities of Atreyu, the boy hero from the lands of the Grass Oceans whose exploits formed the story which drew Bastian into Fantastica to rename the Childlike Empress, and of Xayide, the enchantress who lures Bastian and his party to the castle built like a Seeing Hand, are more acutely realised. In Atreyu and Xayide Bastian confronts Jungian images of himself, his own light and dark side, respectively the *animus* and the *anima* of Jungian psychology, the male and female elements within himself. These must be confronted for an individual to become whole; and perhaps it is not so surprising that Bastian is drawn to the evil Xayide, accepting her flatteries and refusing to see that her purposes are entirely manipulative and self-serving. Eventually, however, Bastian begins to realise his predicament: when imagination robs someone of an appreciation for the real world, it becomes mere fancy, or worse, a lie. After further adventures, Bastian meets Dame Eyola, who nurtures him in the allegorically-named House of Change.

If Xayide is the image of the dark anima, Dame Eyola is the contrasting figure of the nurturing, healing anima. She is very close to the Grandmother figures of George MacDonald's children books with her kindness and in the way she offers gentle moral guidance. With the fruit which grows out of her body, she feeds Bastian; she is here the benevolent Mother Nature, a point she makes clear when Bastian expresses his embarrassment at eating the fruit she takes from her hat and her clothes:

> . . .'I don't know,' he said, 'is it all right to eat something that comes out of somebody?'
> 'Why not?' asked Dame Eyola. 'Babies drink milk that comes out of their mothers. There's nothing better.' (361)

When Bastian protests further that babies suckle "only when they're very little," Dame Eyola merely counters with, ". . . you'll just have to get to be very little again, my dear boy" (361). There are very strong allusions here to the biblical message that "unless you become like little

children, you shall not enter the kingdom of heaven" (Matthew 18:3).
Bastian reverts to a pseudo-babyhood under Dame Eyola's care; and is
comforted when he tells her about his adventure in Fantastica, especially
his betrayal of Atreyu while he was deceived by Xayide. He confesses,
"I did everything wrong." Dame Eyola explains that the way he has
chosen, the "way of wishes," is "the long way round," but since his
destiny is to find the fountain from which springs the Water of Life,
"every way that leads there is the right one" (365).

This is very close to C.S. Lewis's assertion that "the dialectic of
desire...would retrieve all mistakes, head you off from all false paths,
and force you...to live through...a sort of ontological proof" (10).
Imagery such as that of the Water of Life and the House of Change
(which is, as Dame Eyola points out, "bigger inside than out" [362])
is undoubtedly metaphysical, and very close to Lewis's own imagery
in the Narnian Chronicles, especially the Stable in *The Last Battle*, which
the Narnians enter as their old world comes to an end outside. Once
inside the Stable, Tirian, The Narnian Prince,

> ...could hardly believe his eyes. There was the blue sky overhead, and grassy country
> spreading as far as he could see in every direction, and his new friends all round him
> laughing.
>
> 'It seems, then,' said Tirian, smiling himself, 'that the Stable seen from within and
> the Stable seen from without are two different places.'
>
> 'Yes,' said the Lord Digory. 'Its inside is bigger than its outside.'
>
> 'Yes,' said Queen Lucy. 'In our world too, a Stable once had something inside it
> that was bigger than our whole world.' (140-141)

While Lewis's allusions are clear, Ende's are much more oblique. The
House of Change has led Bastian to the recognition of a very deep longing
within him which "was different in every way from all his previous
wishes: the longing to be capable of loving" (366-67). The parallels
between Lewis's world and Ende's are closer than a first glance suggests,
since the Stable represents for the Christian Lewis the incarnation of
Christ, the embodiment of Love. If the House of Change is reminiscent
of the Stable, it comes as no surprise that the need for Love should
be made manifest in the little boy who takes refuge within it. Though
not overtly "Christian," avoiding Lewis's Christian didacticism as
skillfully as he avoids Le Guin's insistent Taoist polemic, Ende
nevertheless touches on human need, both psychological and spiritual.
And for Bastian to learn love, he must taste the Water of Life, and take
some of it back to his own world.

From Dame Eyola's care, Bastian ventures forth again to pursue
his final wish. He digs with the old miner, Yor, for Art in the deep
underground recesses of Minroud, and after much effort finds a picture
of his father, though by this time Bastian has lost his memories of his

father and is merely drawn inexplicably to the painting, in which the pictured man is encased in a block of ice. The struggle to mine for pictures has important symbolic implications, one being the Jungian notion of exploring the subconscious, and another being the spiritual value of art. This last wish has cost Bastian everything: by now he no longer has a name. This is perhaps the bleakest moment of the book; the little boy who took refuge in the school attic with his magical book has had to learn hard lessons through his experience with the world of Fantastica.

That, of course, is part of the value of Fantasy. Derided by some as "escapist nonsense," Fantasy offers sometimes uncomfortable and very often quite painful encounters as readers see in metaphorical mirrors, which it is the business of fantasy to construct, images of themselves. Fantasy is a confrontationist literature, and its message is often uncompromisingly harsh. But even at this bleak moment there is an echo of Dame Eyola's promise: "Nothing is lost. Everything is transformed" (366). Bastian has, however, one more thing to lose: the amulet Auryn, given to him by the Childlike Empress. Almost thwarted in the final stages of his quest by his own foolish creation, the Shlamoofs, Bastian is near despair when he encounters Atreyu and the Luckdragon. The precious picture has been broken, and Bastian's chances of breaking free from the now unbearable fantasies of Fantastica seem very remote. But in one last act of self-surrender, he returns the amulet to Atreyu.

As he does so, the amulet becomes alive, the two snakes encircling a fountain which contains the Water of Life. Bastian farewells his friends, charging Atreyu with the task of "finishing all the stories" Bastian has left behind, and returns to the "real" world, to his distraught father who has been searching overnight for his son, and to the business of living. He tells his story to his father, adding sadly that he has spilled the Water of Life which he had tried so hard to bring back:

> It was almost dark in the kitchen. His father sat motionless. Bastian stood up and switched on the light. And then he saw something he had never seen before.
> He saw tears in his father's eyes.
> And he knew that he had brought him the Water of Life after all. (391)

The Water of Life turns out to be, after all, a story. A story of a little boy's adventures in a fantasy land, adventures that lead him back to his father's affections. In those adventures, Bastian has learned courage and faithfulness (or at least, he learns that he already has those qualities, rather like the lion in *The Wizard of Oz*), and most importantly, he learned how to receive and to give love. Stories have the power to influence growth and change in the reader, to touch them emotionally, psychologically and spiritually. In that respect, this story is very like what Douglas Thorpe sees as "Blakean dream" of Dorothy in the film world of Oz, where the realm of Fantasy is shown in colour against the black and white of mundane reality. Douglas Thorpe sees Dorothy's dream of Oz in a way which might be applied to Bastian's adventures in Fantastica:

> Stories such as these begin where Jesus also began: transforming the self by transforming the narrative the way we see ourselves. The story has momentarily reshaped our lives, now it's up to us to live according to that shape.
>
> ...The new shape of our lives is not just personal; it is seen as ultimate and so its demand is also ethical. Shelley saw this connection between the imagination, love, morals, and politics a century and a half ago...(13-14)

Much of what Thorpe writes about the film version of *The Wizard of Oz* holds true also for *The Neverending Story*. Frank Baum's children's story was written in 1900, in an attempt to bring "wonderment and joy" to its readers; Michael Ende's novel written in 1979 has the same purpose in a world even then given to pragmatics, rampant capitalism and technology. As Thorpe writes,

> Early in Blake's career he set down the principles that would guide all his work, concluding (in 'There is No Natural Religion') that 'God becomes as we are that we might be as He is.' Since in Blake 'we become what we behold,' we must behold God in our fallen world in order to become God. (14)

And to "become God," or at least to become what Tolkien would call the Sub-Creator, "we must be born again": Bastian is reborn through the fountain in Fantastica; his father is reborn through his healing tears. For the God of this book is the story-telling God, very close to the God of Brian Wicker's *The Story Shaped World*, where God becomes a character in a book (The Bible) so that humans might better understand not only him, but also themselves (Wicker 71-106). There is no doubt then, that despite the recurring threat of the Nothing, the stalking of the dark shadow of the Gmork, the being "without a world," despite the misuse of wishes and the betrayal of friends, the world of Fantastica is a place of healing.

It is a place of escape, of course. But it is an escape into something, not an escape from something. It is an escape into self-discovery, self-surrender, healing and wholeness—and these are things intended not for self-gratification, but to bring back and share with others. Ende draws on many sources for his ultimate message, but it is a message of hope. It fulfills all the potential of the "Fantastical Mode" of storytelling, which, as C.S. Lewis writes, has the power

> ...to generalise while remaining concrete, to present in palpable form not concepts or even experiences but whole classes of experience, and to throw off irrelevancies. But

at its best it can do more; it can give us experiences we have never had and thus, instead of "commenting on life," can add to it. (Lewis 74-75)

The Neverending Story is a profoundly Romantic, profoundly religious story. It is never lost in didacticism, and yet it offers very powerful symbolism for those who are willing to decode it. It does not shrink from scepticism (is there, perhaps, some ironic pun of the negating of the author's name in the *title*?) but it articulates hope through the act of self-giving. This is a text which, as Stephen Prickett has said of the poetry of the Romantics, encourages readers to "change the way they experience life."

Chapter Nine
Some American Fables, Sardonic and Satirical

If you prick us, do we not bleed? If you tickle us,
do we not laugh? If you poison us, do we not die?
and if you wrong us, shall we not revenge?
William Shakespeare, *The Merchant of Venice* [III:i:69]

There is probably no nation on Earth—except perhaps the Vatican and Ireland—in which religious issues count for as much as they do in the United States of America. Although constitutionally there is separation of church and state, the historical fact that the country was founded by members of a religious group seeking freedom of worship pervades the culture of the nation. Thanksgiving Day commemorates the landing of the Pilgrim fathers and the dawning of a religious tradition; and the fact that so many religious sects of various kinds and varying degrees of rationality have been spawned in that country attests to the perceived depth of both religious faith and religious freedom.

It is something of a surprise, then, to discover in the literature of the United States a deep scepticism, and nowhere is this more acutely found than in the fantasy writings of the twentieth century. Of course, there are fantasy writers who have a specifically Christian message to impart; John White's *The Tower of Geburah* is a fairly unremarkable imitation of C.S. Lewis's Narnian stories, and Madeleine L'Engle, whose children's books will be discussed in the following chapter, certainly writes from a Christian perspective. But writers in what Raymond M. Olderman calls the "fabulist" tradition (187-88) distance themselves considerably from any articulation of religious belief and indeed look upon life as essentially random and meaningless. Olderman's study is concerned with American literature of the nineteen sixties and he discusses Kurt Vonnegut Jr. and Peter Beagle in the context of the political, social and cultural concerns of that era. However, scepticism is apparent in American literature long before the sixties; in *The Wizard of Oz*, for example, the magic and wonderment build up to the anticlimactic moment when the Wizard reveals himself to be merely a very ordinary man. It comes as no surprise, then, that readers should find the same biting satire to be found in the works of Vonnegut and Beagle, also in the fantasies of James Thurber. And essentially the underlying message in Thurber's writings is the same as in those of his two compatriots: that in what seems to be a meaningless world, it is the role of the writer to give readers something to live for and to hope in. That being the case, it is quite clear that the sceptical American fabulists see the author in precisely the same way as do the English Romantics: adopting the priestly role of giving wise and kindly advice to a despairing world, by "sanctifying," as it were, the faculty of human Imagination, and by the articulation of hope.

Possibly the best known of Thurber's fables is his brief vignette "The Unicorn in the Garden." It is a simple tale of a man who sees a unicorn in his garden, goes upstairs to tell his wife (who is still in bed) and is greeted with disbelief and derision. The wife, a thoroughly nasty though eminently pragmatic person, summons the police and a psychiatrist to deal with her husband's sudden insanity, but of course under questioning, her husband (obviously used to years of agreeing with his wife in the best "yes, dear" tradition) denies that he has seen the unicorn and it is the wife who is carried away, protesting furiously, in the straightjacket.

Of course this fable can be read as a commentary on American "momism," and indeed "momism" becomes itself a metaphor for political and corporate machinations as well—in, for example, Ken Kesey's *One Flew Over the Cuckoo's Nest*, where the Head Nurse, Ratched, obviously symbolises the rigid, unimaginative and pragmatic conformity imposed upon American society. In America, during the McCarthy era, it was possible to be charged with "Un-American" activities, the suggestion being that nationality conferred a kind of political and ethical uniformity upon citizens. The asylum over which Nurse Ratched presides is a model of American society in which there is no room for the imaginative exploits of the individualistic McMurphy: this is a book, Olderman says, which is "closely tied to American tradition" (48).

Thurber's "The Unicorn in the Garden" sets up a paradigm, not only for Kesey's novel but also for those of Vonnegut and Beagle. His fable is likely to be denounced in these enlightened times as "sexist"; and it must be said that American "Momism" typified the times before the women's movement became as articulate and politically influential as it is today. "Momism" was a subversive method of empowering the powerless, but it provided Thurber with the focus for many of his bitter and ironic comments upon the society in which he lived. In this fable, the wife clearly represents pragmatism and rationality; but with that she also denies the reach of the imagination and the sense of wonder that is available in the world of nature as represented by the garden in the fresh light of a new day.

The husband is a simple sort of chap, a man who can see with the eyes of wonder and who can offer to share that sense of delight with his wife. The subtext of this fable seems to be that this is an often-played scenario. The wife is tired of her husband's crazy imaginings, and he seems wearily accustomed to giving in to her insistence upon rationality and order, an insistence which makes life, for him, a kind of prison. Eventually, by the very dogmatism which has imprisoned him, he is set free: she is the one who has lost touch with sanity by denying the world of the Imagination.

There are resonances here with Charles Dickens's *Hard Times*, where Sissy Jupe, the circus girl, is soundly condemned by Gradgrind for indulging in imaginative pursuits. Something of the Utilitarianism of the British Victorian age seems to have permeated into the technological climate of twentieth century America, and Thurber's fable suggests that there is a role for the "Sissy Jupes," male or female, to play in society by reinstating an appreciation of imaginative wonder and delight.

Underscoring this symbolic point in the fable is the notion of the writer as the moral guide, the priest, as it were, of the imagination. The writer has constructed this tale to bring "release to the captives," that is, to liberate those who can release the imagination in a creative and healing way from the constriction and restraints of the conformist, pragmatic, and technological society which sees no value, or only madness, in the imagination and the world of wonder.

Interestingly, Thurber uses language carefully to construct his polemical point; the woman's reactions are described succinctly with negatively loaded words: "She opened one unfriendly eye"; "the woman...looked at him coldly"; "there was a gloat in her eye." Her own utterances are similarly weighted: "You are a booby...and I am going to have to put you in the booby-hatch." The husband, however, "had never liked the words 'booby' and 'booby hatch'...and liked them even less on a shining morning when there was a unicorn in the garden" (268). The contrast between the world of nature and the rigid structure of mundanity and pragmatism is very clear, and readerly sympathies are directed to the husband. There is not much hope for the unimaginative, Thurber suggests; they are straightjacketed in their beliefs and behaviour and cannot escape. The husband does not "buck the system"; under the police and psychiatrist's interrogation, he toes the party line and agrees, as he has learned to do, with his wife. The very system by which she had hoped to entrap him has in fact trapped her. Hope lies in the exercise of the imagination, and by letting the system entrap those who do not have eyes to behold simple wonders created by the imagination. The appearance of the unicorn in the garden is, I feel sure, meant to be seen as the creative faculty of the imagination inspired by the world of nature, and in this Thurber is close to Coleridge and the Romantic tradition.

It comes as no surprise to learn, then, that Thurber also turned his hand to fairy stories for children, and *The Thirteen Clocks* is perhaps the best known, although recent editions of this story also include his *The Wonderful O*. In *The Thirteen Clocks* there are all the elements of the fairy tale—but all of them are slightly parodied, and all through Thurber has inserted sly jokes: the prince who comes to town disguised as a minstrel "called himself Xingu, which was not his name, and dangerous, since the name began with X—and still does" (10). [The Duke has vowed to slay anyone with a name beginning with X.] The minstrel is "a thing of shreds and patches"—a quotation from Gilbert and Sullivan's opera, *The Mikado,* and the Duke is given to slitting people "from their guggle to their zatch" (12). As well as the comic play Thurber indulges in, there is also some doubt about the power of magic. The Golux, for example, who plays the role defined by Vladimir Propp as "the helper" (25-64) is not terribly reassuring:

[The minstrel said:] 'I place my faith in you, and where you lead, I follow.'
'Not so fast,' the Golux said. 'Half the places I have been to, never were. I make things up. Half the things I say are there cannot be found. When I was young I told a tale of buried gold, and men from leagues around dug in the woods. I dug myself.'
    'But why?'
    'I thought the tale of treasure might be true.'
    'You said you made it up.'
    'I know I did, but then I didn't know I had. I forget things, too.' The minstrel felt a vague uncertainty. 'I make mistakes, but I am on the side of Good,' the Golux said, 'by accident and happenchance. I had high hopes of being Evil when I was two, but in my youth I came upon a firefly burning in a spider's web. I saved the victim's life.'
(20)

This is subversive prose disguised as comedy. Not only are the powers of good, represented by the Golux, not very reliable, but the concepts of good and evil are seen as matters of chance rather than of choice. And even the "good deed" to which the Golux refers as his moment of destiny is subverted; it is not the firefly who is saved but the spider: "The blinking arsonist had set the web on fire" (*loc.cit.*).

Nevertheless, since the Golux is there by way of magical help, the minstrel (who turns out to be Prince Zorn of Zorna, and who has been given by the Duke a series of impossible tasks to perform in order to win the hand of the Duke's niece, Saralinda) sets off with the Golux to find the old woman, Hagga, whose tears turn to precious gems. They cannot make Hagga weep; the alternative is to make her laugh, although the gems created in this way will not last. They tell jokes and recite limericks; but nothing conventional works. When Hagga finally begins to laugh, it is at nothing immediately apparent; the tale's self-reflexivity suggests that she is simply laughing at the absurdity being created within the narrative itself. The Golux, referred to even by the Duke as "You Golux *ex machina*," offers comments upon the developments in the plot, and others appear as authorial comment, often to subvert the progress of the narrative and indeed even to subvert the "happy ending":

> The two white horses snorted snowy mist in the cool green glade that led down to the harbour. A fair wind stood for Yarrow and, looking far to sea, the Princess Saralinda thought she saw, as people often think they see, on clear and windless days, the distant shining shores of Ever After. Your guess is quite as good as mine (there are a lot of things that shine) but I have always thought she did, and I will always think so. (75)

As the gently mocking tone suggests, the value of fairy stories is not so much the value they place on magic, but on the way they inspire the development of the imagination. In "a lot of things that shine" there can be a vision of "happy ever after," but it is a construct of the imagination and its consolation is the escape that it provides, not the assurance or the certainties it establishes. Indeed this passage is full of uncertainties; the happiness of the ending depends very much on the reader's suspension of disbelief—or perhaps even more, the determination to hope that the Prince and his bride "lived happily ever after."

It is, perhaps, a further example of textual subversion that one finds that this is only the penultimate episode. In an epilogue, we find the Duke disillusioned because his gems have turned back to tears. He summons the Todal, a gruesome monster to whom he has fed his enemies, and offers himself to it in a passage the language of which is particularly unpleasant:

> 'Come on, you blob of glup,' the cold Duke roared. 'You may frighten octopi to death, you gibbous spawn of hate and thunder, but not the Duke of Coffin Castle!' He sneered. 'Now that my precious gems have turned to thlup, living on, alone and cold, is not my fondest wish! On guard, you musty sofa!' The Todal gleeped. There was a stifled shriek and silence. (77)

This story, then, appears to deny the operation of the supernatural, even in the form of magic; the help of the Golux is at best sporadic and unreliable. But to counter this scepticism, there is an undoubted celebration of life, and with it the power of the imagination to make life worthwhile. The cold Duke is apparently an image of Death-in-Life, and this Coleridgean figure is very clearly associated with manipulation, power, and avarice. The final devouring of the Duke by his own vile monster seems appropriate, since having dealt death to so many, he must, at the moment of failure, deal death to himself. And even this death is treated in Thurber's mocking style; there is an echo in the castle, after the Duke has been devoured, of Hagga's laughter.

And it is with this final mockery that the story concludes. It is true that the elements of self-reflexivity and self-mockery that Thurber encodes into the tale have not spoilt the enjoyment of its readers; indeed its popularity (as evidenced by several reprints) suggests that readers enjoy the joke. Again we see the role of the author priest, however; the gift Thurber gives is laughter, the recognition of age-old fairy tale elements being parodied and mocked, the usual certainties ("good fairy," "wicked witch") being undermined by chance and happenstance. But Thurber articulates hope in that he offers a celebration of life, something to delight in, the reach of the imagination as a kind of "blessing" in an otherwise discouraging world.

The value of literature and the way it works to activate the imagination, to affirm individuality and to celebrate life, is the concern of the fantasy-fable *The Wonderful O*. The plot deals with the imposition of linguistic barbarisms upon an unsuspecting populace by two sailors who are hunting for treasure. Black and Littlejack seek to plunder a "far and distant island" where they believe there is a map to show the whereabouts of buried jewels. The residents deny any knowledge of the map, but the two piratical sailors wreck the town, convinced that there is treasure there somewhere. Their vandalism uncovers only things spelled with the letter O, and in their frustration and rage, the two ban the use of any word containing an O. In an Orwellian enterprise, the loss of one letter effectively undermines any sense of meaning in a great number of words:

> And so the locksmith became a lcksmith, and the bootmaker a btmaker, and people whispered like conspirators when they said the names. *Love's Labour's Lost* and *Mother Goose* flattened out like a pricked balloon. Books were bks and Robinhood was Rbinhd... It was impossible to read "cockadoodledoo" aloud, and parents gave up reading to their children, and some gave up reading altogether... (88-89)

This is Orwell's linguistic nightmare taken a step further; the abolition, not of certain words, but of simply one letter from the language removes the possibility of developing the imagination since the act of reading becomes impossible. But Thurber takes his point further: not only are the words containing O banned, but objects and occupations described by words containing an O are also proscribed:

> ...before they were through they had torn down colleges and destroyed many a book and tome and volume, and globe and blackboard and pointer, and banished professors, assistant professors, scholars, tutors and instructors. There was no one left to translate English into English. (104)

Thurber obviously has in mind certain corruptions of the language, for he has his character Hyde remark that, while the missing O has made language "a messy lessness, whose meaninglessness none the less attracts...more and more...[p]eople often have respect for what they cannot comprehend" (116). This is, ironically, the charge that is often laid against post-structuralist theoretical writings—that they are obscurantist, that, as David Lodge observes, "the age of theory" challenges humanistic values "in an arcane and jargon-ridden form of discourse that can only be understood after a long and strenuous initiation, if at all" (Lodge 113). Certainly the aims of Thurber's villains in this story are the same as Orwell's Big Brother and Lewis's nasty N.I.C.E.: to rob the language of meaning; and to denude language of meaning is to take away the joy of life: "Take the F from life and you have lie," Hyde remarks (117). The hope Thurber articulates is that which lies in language and literature. Black and Littlejack are haunted and hunted by figures out of song and story. They are indestructible, because although "Books can be burned" as Black croaks, Andreas, leader of the islanders, reminds him, "They have a way of rising out of ashes" (131).

Moreover, the treasure when it is found, is not a collection of jewels but a word: "Freedom." And with the treasure of freedom in their possession, the islanders defeat the pirates and restore their language. But Thurber is not content merely to leave the story happily complete there. He issues a warning that the language must be safeguarded diligently; it is not enough simply to be congratulatory of past victories. The islanders erect a monument to the letter O, but years later, people comment on the strangeness of having a statue of a circle. "Was it a battle? And did we win?" a little girl asks. An old man tells her that the victory was indeed a famous one. But he cannot remember what it was about.

This ending effectively undermines the element of certainty suggested by the return of the letter O. Attacks on the language can be overlooked or forgotten; they can occur at any time and in any context. When language is eroded in any way—either through Newspeak or by the simple operation of removing one letter from the alphabet, the tradition of language and literature, indeed the whole of life, is under threat. And yet it is in literature, specifically in fairy tale, myth, fantasy and fable, that there is hope for the language. For in them is enshrined the wealth of the imagination, from which comes the ability to find in mundane existence things to wonder at and to delight in. Thurber's role is very clearly that of prophet/priest in this story; he defends the canon of literature and the imaginative reach of language from those who would pirate and despoil it. He offers no overtly religious solutions to the problems of life, and yet his solutions are profoundly religious. Words, stories and songs are not merely the operation of the human imagination. They are also the business of the world's great sacred books.

Kurt Vonnegut savagely lampoons the language of religion in his bitingly satirical novel *Cat's Cradle*, although he recognises the consolatory potency of story and myth, words and songs. Against a background of human misery, exploitation, failure and greed, he depicts the religion of Bokononism, which offers gentle snippets of wisdom such as "Peculiar travel suggestions are dancing lessons from God" (44), and an explanation of the purpose of individual lives by proposing the notion of a network of relationships called a "karass." The notion of the karass is celebrated in one of the calypsos which serve Bokononists in the place of psalms and hymns:

Oh, a sleeping drunkard
Up in Central Park,
And a lion-hunter
In the jungle dark,
And a Chinese dentist,
And a British queen—
All fit together
In the same machine. (8)

Against the background of a world without much to offer in the line of genuine faith or hope for the future, whether his scepticism takes the form of grotesque Americans taking "culture" abroad, or of the miserable, exploited residents of the barren island of San Lorenzo, ruled by a dictator called Papa Monzano, Vonnegut explores the implications of the randomness and meaninglessness of human existence. His portrayal of the American couple from Indiana ("Hoosiers") serves to indict American Fascism. H. Lowe Crosby is a bicycle manufacturer who has despaired of the impact of the union movements upon his business and is heading for San Lorenzo where the people are "poor enough and scared enough and ignorant enough" to appreciate a job in his factory. His indictment of the union movement is a typical extremist, redneck view:

Christ, back in Chicago, we don't make bicycles any more. It's all human relations now. The eggheads sit around trying to figure out new ways for everybody to be happy. Nobody can get fired, no matter what; and if somebody does accidentally make a bicycle, the union accuses us of cruel and inhuman practices and the government confiscates the bicycle for back taxes and gives it to a blind man in Afghanistan. (59)

It is clear from this statement, however, that in spite of Crosby's exaggerations and extremism, Vonnegut is also taking a shot at most of the institutions—including unions and left wing politics—which make up the American way of life. He calls them elsewhere "granfalloons" and likens them to the "skin of a pricked balloon." They include "the Communist Party, the Daughters of the American Revolution, the General Electric Company, the International Order of Oddfellows—and any nation, any time, anywhere" (61). These "granfalloons" represent various means by which people strive to "belong" to the networks which in turn give their lives some illusion of meaning and purpose. Vonnegut's point is that there *is* no meaning and purpose; but humans need to live as though there were.

Readers can feel comfortable with reading this as a nihilistic text, because we are warned that "nothing in this book is true," and in the early chapters, the narrator, John, decides that he is not "meant" to be a nihilist, after an itinerant poet, Krebs, has stayed in John's flat and left it filthy, having also killed John's cat and scrawled messages in excrement upon the kitchen floor. But John's sardonic tone as he relates the events which lead up to the destruction of the planet by ice-nine betrays his—and Vonnegut's—nihilism. For although Vonnegut (or Jonah/John) warns readers in Chapter Four that "Anyone unable to understand how a useful religion can be founded on lies will not understand this book either" (9), there is no doubt that the religion of Bokononism is indeed "useful"—it consoles the tragic citizens of San Lorenzo, and it serves to highlight very acutely the placebo effect of religion in general. There is nothing to believe in, nothing to hope for, nothing but random fate and meaninglessness. The determinism of Bokononism ("As it happened—'as it was *supposed* to happen'," Bokonon would say [56]) effectively mocks and deconstructs any notion of destiny or determinism, since the plot is not much more than a series of outlandish co-incidences strung together with sardonic commentary.

If religion is ridiculed, so also is science in the form of the Hoenikker family. Felix Hoenikker, the father, is seen as a highly neurotic, introverted workaholic with severe tunnel vision, unable to think or care about the ramifications of his inventions, the atom bomb and ice-nine. The children are all mutants of some kind. Newt is, as his name suggests, a midget (perhaps there is an oblique allusion to the relationship between newts and salamanders; while there is an additional application for the word salamander to a fiery poker used to detonate gunpowder. Newt, like his siblings, carries with him a thermos flask containing the lethal ice-nine). Angela, Newt's sister, is a giantess; while Frank is emotionally disturbed. All three "buy" the affections of members of the opposite sex by selling the secrets of ice-nine; all three are in various ways, traitors. And the implicit suggestion in the novel is, of course, that to misuse science destructively either through atomic energy or ice-nine (an almost diametrically opposite form of destructive agency) is itself treachery to one's kind.

It is Ambassador Minton, I believe, who articulates hope in this despairing novel. Minton is, perhaps, an ambassador for humanity as a whole, and although his message is delivered only a few seconds before his violent death, nevertheless his death serves to emphasise the message rather than to displace or negate it. The message is simple and profound:

'...Think of people...
'And children murdered in war...
'And any country at all.
'Think of peace.
'Think of brotherly love.
'Think of plenty.
'Think of what a paradise this world would be if men were kind and wise.
'As stupid and vicious as men are, this is a lovely day...' (160)

The book condemns the inhumanity of humans to each other, but it suggests that despite the meaninglessness of existence, it can be made a "paradise" even in a Waste Land like San Lorenzo by the operation of human kindness and generosity. In other words, Vonnegut articulates the sense of the Australian [Anglican] Prayer Book: "that we may share with justice the resources of the earth, work together in trust, and seek the common good" (141). Both Vonnegut and the Prayer Book offer ideals to strive for; both share the same awareness of the world's inexplicable tragedies and miseries. As I prepare this manuscript, there has been in Queensland (where I live) an area greater than that of all Great Britain submerged by the most catastrophic floods in history. Whole towns have been almost annihilated. The floods have also devastated New South Wales, where a major city is still recovering from a destructive earthquake. And a light plane carrying members of a provincial town council has crashed, killing them all. It is very difficult to find answers to the perplexities raised by these events. There would hardly be a person who has not been affected by them in some way. It may not be "ice-nine," but to the people involved the distinction would be blurred; what can religion offer in the face of such suffering? Vonnegut is concerned with questions such as these, and his first novel, *Slaughterhouse Five*, deals in particular with the bombing of Dresden. In every instance, however, he seizes upon some human tragedy and attempts to make sense of it; failing that, he seeks to impose on it some way of coping, some way of sustaining through tragedy human integrity and hope.

The hope he offers is imaginative: the writer can provide escape from the tragedies and offer at least some diversion. As Jerome Klinkowitz comments, Vonnegut intends readers to "take hope in the artifice...for there...is where truth and meaning lie" (54). It isn't much, but literature—"lies"—might make us "brave and kind and healthy and happy" (6). Vonnegut articulates the role of the writer tongue-in-cheek,

but nevertheless quite emphatically, when he has his narrator, Jonah/
John, discussing the possibility of a writers' strike with hotel owner
Philip Castle. Castle says:

> 'I'm thinking of calling a general strike of all writers until mankind finally comes
> to its senses. Would you support it?'

To which John replies:

> 'Do writers have a right to strike? That would be like police or firemen walking
> out.'
> 'Or the college professors.'
> 'Or the college professors,' I agreed. I shook my head. 'No, I don't think my conscience
> would let me support a strike like that. When a man becomes a writer, I think he takes
> on a sacred obligation to produce beauty and enlightenment and comfort at top speed.'
> 'I just can't help thinking what a real shaking up it would give people if, all of
> a sudden, there were no new books, new plays, new histories, new poems...'
> 'And how proud would you be when people started dying like flies?' I demanded.
> 'They'd die more like mad dogs, I think—snarling and snapping at each other and
> biting their own tails.'
> I turned to Castle the elder. 'Sir, how does a man die when he's deprived of the consolations
> of literature?'
> 'In one of two ways,' he said, 'putrescence of the heart or atrophy of the nervous
> system.' (145)

This is, I believe, the real climax of the book, the point at which
the satire gives way to the articulation of the real argument behind the
book's powerful polemic. As Wayne C. Booth has pointed out, irony
depends upon the necessity to reveal at some time that the text is to
be read ironically, and that there is a message to be decoded at a non-
ironic level.[1] While Vonnegut makes his irony and satire eminently easy
to decode, he nevertheless breaks his own code of reading into the world
as a text mere meaninglessness, and provides in his own text the ulterior
meaning that dealing with life's perplexities is possible because of the
"consolations of literature." In today's technological world, writers do
indeed churn out "beauty and enlightenment and comfort at top speed."

In short, however, Vonnegut is suggesting a "sacred" role for the
writer, the guardian of the Imagination, the prophet who warns of
impending destruction. Jonah, after all, was noted for having the task
of proclaiming God's wrath to Nineveh, and demanding that the city
repent. Somewhat to his chagrin, it did, and disaster did not overtake
the city. The nickname "Jonah" for the book's narrator, and the whale-
like shape of San Lorenzo, seems to suggest allegorically that Vonnegut
is issuing this warning from "the whale's belly" as it were, in the hope
that readers will "repent" of the institutions and machinations which
will eventually destroy the world and all humanity. This is very clearly

a book in which the sceptical author exploits the displacement of religious language into literature and especially into fantasy. And while this novel too is often classified as "science fictional," it is, I believe, by virtue of its allegorical impetus also fantasy. It uses, as Olderman notes, the imagery of the Waste Land; but while Olderman sees Bokonon as the Fisher King with his consoling message, Bokonon is really only another author whose religion is made up of the business of literature—story, myth, song. And here religion and literature, in this modern day, converge; and it is through the religious function of literature—its ability to comfort and console, to amuse and to enlighten—that Vonnegut offers hope.

The hope he offers is twofold. Firstly, through literature, readers can "escape" briefly the terrors and tragedies of life; secondly, if they heed the prophetic warnings of the author-priests (their duty is "sacred," as Jonah insists) it may be that the world will not suffer annihilation and destruction at the hands of human beings.

Peter Beagle takes up the same point, but with a different emphasis. Like Vonnegut, his hope is constructed from illusion, but illusions are themselves a matter of choice. Some add only to the existential angst already abroad; but others, symbolised by the unicorn in his novel *The Last Unicorn*, lend to the Waste Land of the world a sense of wonder.[2]

The evils that Beagle perceives in the world about him are not perhaps as dramatically catastrophic as those encapsulated in Vonnegut's grim scenarios; but are more pervasive, and more easily accommodated by an unsuspecting humanity simply because of their lack of drama. Apathy, advertising, and angst are not the stuff of high adventure; and yet they undermine and erode the joy of living by a cancerous colonisation of the human spirit and so are most assuredly "the enemy." That apathy is a major part of the malaise which afflicts the world of *The Last Unicorn* is clear from the unicorn's plaint that humans do not recognise in her and her kind the wonderful and the marvellous:

'How can it be?' she wondered. 'I suppose I could understand it if men had simply forgotten unicorns or if they had changed so that they hated all unicorns now and tried to kill them when they see them. But not to see them at all, to look at them and see something else—...?' (16)

The reason that she is not recognised is, of course, that she is the last of her kind in the world. And although it is clear, as Olderman notes, that the main issue in this novel is the restoration of a sense of wonder to a world which has become a Waste Land without it (Olderman 220-242), there is, I believe, rather more in the symbolism associated with the unicorn which alerts readers to the fact that for Beagle, too, the stuff of myth and fantasy replaces in this age the fundamentals of religious discourse. The Unicorn is, as medieval bestiaries make clear, a symbol for Christ.[3] Beagle (whether consciously or not) exploits the medieval symbolism by recording that with her shimmering horn, the unicorn has "killed dragons with it, and healed a king whose poisoned wound would not close, and knocked down ripe chestnuts for bear cubs" (11). When one recalls that, in the New Testament, the dragon or the worm symbolises Satan, (Revelation 12:9) and the Christian concept of redemption lies in the belief that Christ has defeated Satan; and that healing was part of Christ's earthly ministry, as indeed was the feeding of the multitudes, some parallels intentional or otherwise between Beagle's unicorn and Christ can be drawn. However, the unicorn is female, so there is also some distancing achieved here, although in essence the gender difference does not do violence to the Christian symbolism. At the most basic level, the unicorn as a creature of magic, an "emanation," as it were, of the human Imagination, embodying an almost numinous wonder and awe, is indeed the "savior" of a world denuded of joy.

The realm of advertising and popular music and culture contributes also to the general malaise abroad in Beagle's fictional world. The butterfly converses in snatches of all three, producing a meaningless patter which does nothing to add to the quality of life:

'Death takes what man would keep,' said the butterfly, 'and leaves what man would lose. Blow, wind, and crack your cheeks. I warm my hands before the fire of life and get four-way relief.' (17)

The unicorn is, of course, disappointed at the limited range of the butterfly's communications, but she realizes that "All they know are songs and poetry, and anything else they hear. They mean well, but...they die so soon" (17). There is nothing sustaining in the butterfly's patter, since it is merely a thing of "shreds and patches" so to speak, and not of substance. The unicorn meets Schmendrick the magician in Mommy Fortuna's carnival, a world of poor illusions and great misery. The unicorn is held captive there, caught by two men who think her to be "just an old white mare" (21), to take her place in the carnival which consists of creating illusory magical and monstrous entities. The carnival symbolises life in the busy, technological society where "it takes a cheap carnival witch to make folk recognize a real unicorn" (31). In such a world, it is not surprising to find that a magician is bumbling and ineffectual. Schmendrick is both.

He cannot help the unicorn to escape the Carnival by means of magic. Rather he resorts to the petty human activity of pickpocketing the keys to the cages, and as they escape, the harpy which Mommy Fortuna had imprisoned and constantly derided destroys the rest of the carnival. The unicorn continues her quest for the rest of her kind, and now she is accompanied by Schmendrick the magician, who is on a quest of his own—in search of mortality, by which he can regain his magical powers. The two quests are parallel, and in the intimation that Schmendrick must regain his mortality (a witch has put a spell on him to make him immortal) is the suggestion that, like Ged in Ursula Le Guin's *Earthsea Trilogy*, he must accept the fact of death in order to live more fully. The unicorn, the creature of the Imagination, must accept immortality; only magical creatures can live forever.

Interestingly, there is a very clear allusion to Thurber's tale, "The Unicorn in the Garden," which appears in an episode when a blue jay brings his wife news that he has seen a unicorn. His wife reacts with scorn: "You didn't see any supper, I notice...I hate a man who talks with his mouth empty." The female blue jay attacks her husband: "She was one woman who knew what to do with a slight moral edge" (44). Beagle's story has a very similar message to Thurber's: for both, the realm of the Imagination is morally superior to the mundane world of mere practicality and pragmatics.

The third element of the malaise which has brought about the departure of the unicorns is the existential angst abroad in the world. In this novel, it is symbolized by the Red Bull (Olderman 227-28), a monstrous creature which represents disease, or "dis-ease," a sense of discomfiture in the presence of nameless fears. In the nineteen-sixties, when this book was written, the dominant fear was of the possibility of a nuclear war; later, other fears have displaced that one—fear of the greenhouse effect, fear of the effects of a ruptured ozone layer, fears for the future of the world's green places. Humanity fears what has power over it, and in this novel, the Red Bull very clearly symbolises power—domination, control, festering malevolence: "[The Red Bull] was the color of blood, not the spirning blood of the heart but the blood that stirs under an old wound that never really healed" (82). Whatever kind of force the Bull might represent, there is no doubt that here is the same kind of opposition between "head" and "heart," or "utilitarianism" and "Imagination" that is found in Charles Dickens's *Hard Times*. It is a theme which seems to have found a home in modern America, which wields international political power, and internally the power of the Corporation or of social pressure to conform.

The novel deals with the attempts of Schmendrick and Molly Grue, the woman he finds in the camp of Captain Cully, to help the Unicorn in her quest. To do so, they must conquer the "haggardness" or hopelessness of humanity, as represented by Kind Haggard under whose power and acquisitiveness the unicorns have been imprisoned. Acquisitiveness is a feature of capitalist society, where individuals gather treasures and often store them away uselessly from public viewing and enjoyment. But the mere accumulation of the unicorns brings Haggard neither joy nor satisfaction. Only when he dies are the unicorns released and the "haggardness" of the world healed by their beauty and magic.

It is clear that Beagle believes that humans find hope in a despairing and desolate world through art and literature. The magician, Schmendrick, and the hero, Prince Lir, offer us the consolations of beauty and adventure. Although Prince Lir, in attempting to win the heart of the unicorn, transformed by Schmendrick into a beautiful young woman, attempts many daring deeds, he finds that nothing works. Nevertheless, in his frustration, there is a plaintive humour:

> I have swum four rivers, each in full flood and none less than a mile wide. I have climbed seven mountains never before climbed, slept three nights in the Marsh of the Hanged Men, and walked alive out of that forest where the flowers burn your eyes and the nightingales sing poison. I have ended my betrothal to the princess I had agreed to marry—and if you don't think that was a heroic deed, you don't know her mother. I have vanquished exactly fifteen black knights waiting by fifteen fords in their black pavilions, challenging all who come to pass. And I've long since lost count of the witches in the thorny woods, the giants, the demons disguised as damsels, the glass hills, fatal riddles and terrible tasks; the magic apples, rings, lamps, potions, swords, cloaks, boots, neckties and nightcaps. Not to mention the winged horses, the basilisks and sea serpents and all the rest of the livestock. (106)

Mere adventures as catalogued here, then, do not solve the problem, and yet, as in *The Neverending Story*, they are the "magic" which captures the attention of the reader. Lir is faced with an age-old problem: how to win the woman of his dreams, how to understand her. Molly Grue cannot answer him: "She is a woman, Your Highness, and that's riddle enough" (108). But at last, Prince Lir realizes that he must accept the Princess Amalthea for what she is: a creature of the Imagination; and he lays down his life for her to enable her to become a unicorn again. Prince Lir understands the power of stories, and he knows what readers expect:

> The true secret of being a hero [in a story] lies in knowing the order of things...Things must happen when it is time for them to happen...The happy ending cannot come in the middle of the story. (145)

Stories, like religious observances, are reassuringly ritualistic. There are certain roles for characters to play. "Wizards make no difference so they say that nothing does," Prince Lir observes, "but heroes are meant to die for unicorns" (152). There is, even in a world where magic does not seem to make a difference, a role for heroes—for artists and writers who are willing to risk ridicule and derision for daring to maintain a sense of the marvellous in the writing of fantasy. Beagle's happy ending is not so much that the various quests are fulfilled, but that there will be another story: Schmendrick and Molly "went away together, out of this story and into another" (168). Though Beagle does not attempt to address religious issues, he nevertheless sees the same spiritual potency in literature, and in particular the literature of fantasy, as Tolkien, Ende, Thurber and Vonnegut. In particular, Beagle offers a kind of "neverending story" as his characters head off, not into the sunset, but into another story.

The magic by which the Waste Land is healed is not that of magicians or of wizards, but that of the story tellers who keep alive the magical and the marvellous. The human spirit depends for its survival on the telling of stories, and in stories such as this are the messages, the prophecies perhaps, which inform readers of the possibilities made available by the exercise of the imagination. Like the other fantasists dealt with in this study, Beagle echoes the Romantics, who saw in the imagination the means of participating in a quasi-divine creative and healing act. The American writers discussed in this chapter all celebrate the Imagination, and all recognize in stories the kind of spiritual, psychological and emotional comfort which imbues the world's sacred texts with enduring power. And in the very *act* of writing their stories, the authors of these fantasies appropriate the language of religion and the functions of the prophet/priest, to articulate hope for their readers and for all humanity.

Chapter Ten
Transcending Time and Space:
Fantasy for Children

We are the music-makers
And we are the dreamers of dreams,
Wandering by lone sea-breakers,
And sitting by desolate streams;
World-losers and world-forsakers,
On whom the pale moon gleams:
Yet we are the movers and shakers
Of the world forever, it seems.

Arthur O'Shaughnessy, 'Ode'

There is in juvenile fantasy a recurring theme of the rise of the forces of evil which must be faced and fought by young people who possess special insights or special powers. In most juvenile fantasies, adults are merely supernumeraries—seen either as hindrances, to be somehow removed from the business of the plot, or as co-conspirators— what Vladimir Propp calls "helpers" (84-86)—or very often as the emissaries of evil.

The recurring theme of the intrusion of evil into the lives of children is in and of itself deeply sceptical; no sooner has one seen evil defeated in one novel than one finds it as powerful and malignant as ever on the pages of another. And despite what seems to be a conventional practice of closure in children's fantasies, there is often in fact a sceptical undermining of closure. Other strategies are used to articulate hope; most generally these can be seen in the implicit promise that in every age there will emerge the right person with the magical background or supernatural insights to combat evil.

Children's fantasies of this kind most closely resemble the fairy tale, and in them it is possible to see at least in part the realisation of Tolkien's formula of "Recovery, Escape and Consolation" (50-61). How completely this formula is realised varies from text to text and from author to author, although in children's fantasies no less than in adults', the operation of deep scepticism can be observed together with the subversion of any notion of absolutist faith. But in children's literature, rather more than in adult fantasies, the articulation of hope is often resoundingly clear.

It is not surprising to find that among the most popular authors of children's fantasy literature there are several Christians, including J.R.R. Tolkien, C.S. Lewis, and Madeleine L'Engle. From such writers readers might feel confident of a reassuring absolutism, but in fact it is offered by none of the three. If Madeleine L'Engle appears to be offering something close to Christian absolutism, it is undermined by the surreality of the plots she develops and by the intrusion of fantastical creatures into the experiences of her child heroes.

Indeed, both the evil which threatens and the hope which is promised in children's fantasy literature are located outside of mundane experience. Plots are either played out in a parallel universe (as in the Narnian Chronicles); or by the intrusion of the supernatural into the mundane world (as in L'Engle's fantasies); or by the intrusion into mundane reality of mythical or "historical" figures from the past, as in Alan Garner's novels, Lucy Boston's *Green Knowe* series and Patricia Wrightson's Australian children's stories. The effect of such remote sitings in these stories is to distance the events in the fictional world from experience in the real world. These are, then, instances of Tolkien's notion of "escape"; not merely escape from the mundane world into fantasy, but escape also from the problematics of mundane existence into a world where children are heroic and can achieve victory over the named and embodied fears which beset them namelessly and without form in real life. This is, of course, what happens to Bastian in *The Neverending Story*, where Ende tries to articulate in fictional form the experiences offered to children in the reading of fantasy, and what Tolkien strives to define in his theoretical essay.

Because fantasy offers children the element of "Escape," as Tolkien puts it, it is not common to find in children's fantasies the kind of world-weariness which pervades much realistic fiction for children, although occasionally it does occur. In many "realistic" novels, children are pitted against more tangible but less easily overcome evils—family breakdown, drug experimentation, sexual deviance or promiscuity in themselves, their friends or their parents, social and economic impoverishment and loneliness. These are certainly problems with which today's children are often confronted in their own lives or in the lives of people close to them, and it may be that children who face such problems in "real life" seek the consolations of fantasy for the sake of psychological wholeness. Identification with the heroes of fantasy might very well provide a sustaining psychological balance for young readers, allowing them to combat the all-too-real problems which they face in the context of mundane existence in symbolic or archetypal form.

So when Bilbo Baggins is visited by Gandalf the wizard who just happens to be "looking for somebody to share an adventure" he is arranging, Bilbo scorns the idea of having adventures: "...nasty disturbing uncomfortable things! Make you late for dinner!" he complains (16). Yet the reader urges Bilbo on to participate in the adventure, since adventures are stories into which readers are drawn— and without adventures, there can be no stories. This, too, is a point taken up by Michael Ende in *The Neverending Story*, when Atreyu must do and dare all manner of tasks in order to bring Bastian into the world of Fantastica. Tolkien's approach is similar, although he simply allows the reader to wait anxiously while Bilbo makes up his pragmatic mind about the worth of venturing away from all that is comfortable and reassuring in order to recover stolen gold from the Dragon, Smaug. There is, as well, a little joke between Tolkien and his readers, for there *is* a story to follow, and there must be an adventure as well.

The plot is, of course, a familiar one, and the adventure takes Bilbo into the dark caverns inhabited by the Gollum, where Bilbo wins, in a duel of riddles, the Ring which makes him invisible. But even in gaining the Ring, and with it Gollum's promise of guidance out of the caverns, there is something amiss. Bilbo's riddle is not a riddle; he does not truly "play the game." At first, of course, he does not intend to deceive the Gollum, since Bilbo is merely murmuring to himself "What have I got in my pocket?" (83). But once Bilbo is aware that the Gollum believes that this is a riddle and part of the game, Bilbo does not volunteer the truth. Already there is a shadow cast upon the character of Bilbo—a shadow which will grow darker yet and be passed on, in *The Lord of the Rings*, to Frodo.

As the adventure progresses, the dragon Smaug is slain by Bard, the captain of a company of archers, people from whom Smaug has stolen treasure and livelihood. There is a dispute between Bard's people and the dwarves over the distribution of the treasure: Bilbo feels responsible, and mourns at the death of the wounded leader of the dwarves, Thorin Oakenshield:

'Farewell, King under the Mountain!' he said. 'This is a bitter adventure, if it must end so, and not a mountain of gold can amend it. . . .' (270)

And immediately following, we learn that Bilbo feels more "sorrow then joy, and he was now weary of his adventure. He was aching in his bones for the homeward journey" (271). But even Bilbo's return home is bittersweet. He is glad to

Look at last on meadows green
And trees and hills [he] long had known

but he discovers that he has been presumed dead, and that his relatives are in the process of disposing of all his goods. Indeed, "the legal bother . . . lasted for years." More than that, the life he returns to is not one of unmitigated bliss:

> . . . Bilbo had lost more than his spoons—he had lost his reputation. It is true that for ever after he remained an elf-friend, and had the honour of dwarves, wizards, and all such folk as ever passed that way; but he was no longer quite respectable. He was in fact held by all the hobbits of the neighbourhood to be 'queer'—except by his nephews and nieces on the Took side, but even they were not encouraged in their friendship by their elders. (285)

Tolkien assures us that Bilbo is "very happy," but the Shire in which he lives is certainly not without problems, the most obvious of which is the greed of Bilbo's relatives, their haste in disposing of his property amongst themselves, and their failure to welcome him back. Although the fact that he has been on adventures which his kinfolk could not share gives Bilbo some enjoyment, and the minor games he plays with the magical Ring (disappearing from unwanted guests) amuse him, there is something wistful in this ending which suggests the change in mood and direction which will follow in *The Lord of the Rings*.

As C.S. Lewis was later to remark, fairy tales such as *The Hobbit* "liberate archetypes which dwell in the collective unconscious, and when we read a good fairy tale we are obeying the old precept 'Know Thyself' " (27). Lewis further suggests that the psychological awakening achieved by the power of archetypal images and patterns in literature may also be provoked by the use in stories of the non-human characters, such as dwarfs, giants and talking beasts:

> I believe these to be at least (for they may have many other sources of power and beauty) an admirable hieroglyphic which conveys psychology, types of character, more briefly than novelistic presentation and to readers whom novelistic presentation could not yet reach. (27)

Certainly, in *The Hobbit* we see human nature "writ small" as it were, and Bilbo, though a hero, is told by Gandalf in the concluding lines of the book, "You are a very fine person, Mr. Baggins, and I am very fond of you; but you are only quite a little fellow in a wide world after all!" (285). And in those few words, Tolkien, through Gandalf, articulates the human condition: we are all "quite little fellows in a wide world," often pitted against forces and circumstances we do not understand. Fortunately for us, in the moments when our faith is challenged and life seems blackest, we can have access to wizards and their wisdom simply by turning the pages of a book. Fantasy literature does not merely articulate hope; it is our hope, the door through which we readers can join in adventures in the land of Faerie.

The involvement of children in the battle between good and evil seems to have the same impetus as Tolkien's use of Hobbits or Halflings, who are "little people." Children, too, are "little people," and perhaps there is, consciously or unconsciously, something of Wordsworth's notion that there is some kind of paradisal innocence still present in children, which is absent in adults. As Wordsworth wrote in his "Intimations of Immortality from Recollections of Early Childhood":

> Our birth is but a sleep and a forgetting:
> The soul that rises with us, our life's star,
> Hath had elsewhere its setting,
> And cometh from afar:
> Not in entire forgetfulness,
> And not in utter nakedness,
> But trailing clouds of glory do we come
> From God, who is our home:
> Heaven lies about us in our infancy! (187)

C.S. Lewis, too, echoed the sense of these lines, that something of heaven's glory comes with us into the world at birth but fades from us as we grow to adulthood. For Lewis, however, this paradisal inheritance leaves the adult wistful and full of yearning, full of the nostalgia he called *Sehnsucht*:

> Often me too the Living voices call
> In many a vulgar and habitual place,
> . . . .
> And some day this will work upon me so
> I shall arise and leave both friends and home
> And over many lands a pilgrim go
> Through alien woods and foam.
> Seeking the last steep edges of the earth
> When I may leap into the gulf of light
> Wherein, before my narrowing self had birth,
>   Part of me lived aright.
>
> ("Our Daily Bread", *Spirits in Bondage* 86-87)

Lewis imbues his children's fantasies with this sense of *Sehnsucht*, and provides for his child characters a parallel universe in which there is a land called Narnia where their adventures take place. But although Lewis was a devout Christian, and although Tolkien felt that the Christian imagery in Lewis's children's books was too obvious and too didactic, there are still elements of scepticism in the Narnian Chronicles, and with each succeeding book, the scepticism grows more intense.

In the first book, *The Lion, the Witch and the Wardrobe*, the element of scepticism arises in the early chapters. In the first instance, Lucy, the youngest of the four Pevensie children who feature in the book, stumbles through a wardrobe in the house where they are staying as evacuees from the air-raids of World War II.   Lucy finds herself in the new, parallel world, and encounters a Faun who behaves in the convention of "good" characters, offering food reminiscent of an English nursery tea, and chats about the world he lives in. His bookshelf presents readers with some amusing titles, especially *Nymphs and Their Ways or Men, Monks and Gamekeepers*, and *A Study in Popular Legend or Is Man a Myth?*

Despite these reassuring elements in the Faun's behaviour and domestic scene, Lucy is dismayed to learn that he is in the pay of the White Witch—a traitor, in fact, waiting for her or someone like her to appear in order to report her presence to the Secret Police. Although Lucy manages to convince the Faun that he is not really a traitor, and he obliges by escorting her back to the lamp-post which marks the threshold between the real and the fantastical worlds, the incident alerts readers to the fact that Narnia is a world where appearances cannot be depended upon, and where what seems good—the White Witch with her supplies of Turkish Delight, for instance—may in fact be evil.

The children, of course, meet the Lion Aslan, the figure who symbolises Christ and who, in the course of the story, effects a kind of salvation for the treacherous Edmund, the younger male Pevensie, and for the world of Narnia, delivering it from the thrall of the White Witch and from permanent winter. They are made Kings and Queens of Narnia and the bliss of their existence in the parallel world can almost be summed up by the nostalgia evoked in Lewis's description of their castle:

The castle of Cair Paravel on its little hill towered up above them; before them were the sands, with rocks and little pools of salt water, and seaweed, and the smell of the sea and long miles of bluish-green waves breaking for ever and ever on the beach. And oh, the cry of the seagulls! Have you heard it? Can you remember? (167)

But the children—and children they still are, despite their sudden maturity in Narnia—must return to the real world, resuming with their old clothes their mundane existence. But this is a puzzling ending; for although there is most certainly a promise that the children will return to Narnia, nothing is said about the fate of the Narnians left suddenly without their Kings and Queens. Moreover, in spite of the wonders of their adventures, they are warned by the Professor who owns the house in which they are staying not to speak about their adventures, "unless [it is to people who have] adventures of the same sort themselves" (173).

The Professor is, we learn in a later book, *The Magician's Nephew*, one of those who have visited Narnia, but apart from him, no other such adventurer is ever encountered. To leave the dignity of royal rule and peace and pleasure and to return to a none-too-inviting mundanity hardly seems to be the happiest of endings. Of course, Lewis makes it clear that there will be other trips to Narnia, but this promise is somewhat subverted by the imposition of the real world upon the visions of the edenic parallel world.

There is further scepticism, too, in the fact that Narnia is not a world without evil; indeed evil enters the world almost at its very creation. It is a world like ours, in which not only humans but also talking animals are faced with choices and who must deal with the manifestations of evil as they arise. One might almost ask why Lewis should bother to transfer the battle between good and evil from this world to a parallel world; but the answer to that must lie in Lewis's own cosmographical vision, in which he sees the medieval structures of the Great Chain of Being and the Ptolomeic Universe as allegories or symbols for supernatural reality. That is not to say that he denied scientific evidence; he takes meticulous care to point out that he is aware of the (then) modern models of the universe, but he writes,

I have made no serious effort to hide the fact that the Old Model delights me as I believe it delighted our ancestors. Few constructions of the imagination seem to me to have combined the splendour, sobriety, and coherence in the same degree. (*The Discarded Image* 216)

It is because of his adherence to this "Old Model" of the universe that Lewis peoples his Narnian world with hierarchical structures and chains of obedience. But even when these are in place, the hierarchical infrastructure of the world is no real safeguard against the onslaughts of evil.

There is something so bleak as to be almost Orwellian in the opening chapter of *The Last Battle*, the last of the Narnian Chronicles. It begins hopelessly, "In the last days of Narnia," a warning which is fulfilled at the end of the book. This is an eschatological vision, a kind of Book of the Apocalypse for Narnia. Religion, or what passes for it in Narnia, has lapsed; belief is at a very low ebb. As the crafty Ape who introduces the story tells his enslaved donkey, Puzzle, "[Aslan] never *does* turn up, you know" (10). And indeed, Aslan does not.

Like Lewis's *That Hideous Strength*, this is almost a political text, for the evils which the Ape perpetrates using the donkey clad in a lionskin to impersonate Aslan, are the evils of a totalitarian regime. Resemblances to Orwell's *Animal Farm* are possibly not fortuitous, for Lewis expressed admiration for Orwell's mythic work in a paper published a few months before *The Last Battle*.[1] The two authors never met, but they were contemporaries, and shared the years of pre-war uncertainty and the fears generated by events leading up to and during World War II. Both had been soldiers, Lewis in World War I and Orwell in the Spanish Civil War, and both would have heard reports of totalitarian brutality from both Nazi and Stalinist states. Both authors denounced totalitarian regimes, the misuse of science, the corruption of language and the eroding of individual rights.

In view of these correspondences between the two authors, it is possible to see some thematic and symbolic relationship between Shift the ape and Orwell's dictator-pig, Napoleon; and Puzzle the donkey and Orwell's horse, Boxer, are also related, if not entirely parallel characters. It is also clear that *The Last Battle* is as much a work of political polemic as *Animal Farm*, though the former is perhaps a little less forceful in its tone, since although both are "fairy-stories"[2] Lewis's book is part of a series written for children.

Despite its intended readership, however, *The Last Battle* relentlessly portrays endless destruction of the natural Narnian environment and erosion of traditional Narnian values in an inescapable analogy with Lewis's own perceptions of the modern, mundane world. The totalitarian control effected by the Ape is both sinister and malevolent, and a readership of the 1990s will immediately identify as evil the environmental destruction over which the Ape presides.[3] For Lewis, the destruction of trees meant also the death of the naiads, the tree spirits who give trees their life, and the fact that the trees are being sold for trade highlights the distorted values of the Ape's system of rule.

There is no doubt that the Ape's regime is totalitarian:

Everybody who can work is going to be made to work in future. Aslan has it all settled with the King of Calormen—the Tisroc, as our...friends the Calormenes call him. All you horses and bulls and donkeys are to be sent down into Calormen to work for your living—pulling and carrying the way horses and such-like do in other countries. And all you digging animals like moles and rabbits and Dwarfs are going down to work in the Tisroc's mines...You'll be paid—very good wages too. That is to say, your pay will be paid into Aslan's treasury and he will use it for everybody's good. (30)

There are certainly overtones of Marxist ideology in the Ape's orders, and the reference to "the Tisroc's mines" suggest the punitive mines of Siberia under Stalinist rule. But in addition to the overtly political agenda being addressed here, Lewis is also acknowledging the evils which have been perpetrated in the name of religion over the centuries. This, perhaps, is an apology for "real" religion, that which is uncorrupted by the influence and acquisitiveness of the world systems in which it has its existence. Theologically, the Ape is an atheist, but he exploits what is left of the faith of the Narnians through his makeshift imitation of Aslan and by citing "Aslan's orders" for each of his cruel innovations.

The real scepticism inherent in this novel is that the Narnians cannot discern the truth; they are gullibly taken in by the posturing of the fake Aslan and his Machiavellian master.

Lewis warns elsewhere against the corruption of Christianity. In his theological essay, "What are we to make of Jesus Christ?", he writes,

> The things [Jesus Christ] says are very different from what any other teacher has said. Others say, 'This is the truth about the universe. This is the way you ought to go,' but He says, 'I am the Truth, and the Way, and the Life.' (160)

Lewis's final Narnian Chronicle, then, appropriates the language of religion to issue warnings about the world, and the political and the spiritual environment of the twentieth century. The pessimism abroad in Narnia can only be dealt with in one way—by the end of the world, by death and then resurrection in Paradise. This is, for the modern reader, "pie in the sky by and by," for Lewis does not offer even the hope he articulates in the adult novel *That Hideous Strength* by having supernatural intervention in the created world of Narnia, whereas in the adult novel he allowed such intervention in the mundane world. So although in one sense, the ending of *The Last Battle* is a happy one, it is also a grim and uncompromising one: the Narnian world is doomed, and by the operation of metaphor and allegory, we may assume our world has upon it the same dire sentence. Of course, there is in the paradisal awakening a real articulation of hope; heaven is seen to be the perfect Platonic Form of which our world is only a Copy, and all things, all relationships and all our hopes and treasures will be restored in the New Narnia, the New Heaven and the New Earth.

Among the best of those who follow Lewis's paradigm for Christian fantasy is the American writer Madeleine L'Engle, whose attitude to science is rather different from that of Lewis. Science forms an integral part of her plots, and the parents of her adventuring children are both scientists—even their mother, who has two Ph.Ds. The family is, however, something of an oddity in its community, for all the children are bright, and Charles Wallace, the youngest, is exceptionally so. It is through Charles Wallace's capacity for "kything" (or telepathic communication) that he and his sister Meg, with whom he is very close, can achieve travel across space and time to right the evils which beset people close to them.

Although L'Engle's books are overtly Christian, the religious imagery is handled with verve and imagination. The three angels in the first book of the Charles Wallace trilogy, *A Wrinkle in Time*, are Mrs. Who, Mrs. Which and Mrs. Whatsit, of whom the latter appears in a "wild garb of shawls and scarves and [an] old tramp's coat and hat" (75).

Mrs. Who is given to quotation, including a cautionary word from Goethe: *"Allwissend bin ich nicht; doch viel ist mir bewisst"*—"I do not know everything, still many things I understand" (89). With the help of these three beings, the children set out across space to rescue their father, who has been experimenting with the "tesseract," a way of folding space, from the disembodied entity which holds him in its power and which also gains power over Charles Wallace. It controls, by making them something like robots, the residents of the planet on which it is situated; they are less than human, merely automatons. Meg is the only one who can rescue Charles Wallace, and only because of her close bond with him. She realizes that the only gift she can give him, the only thing which will free him, is her love. Once she realizes that all she has to do is to love her brother, the evil bondage is broken and the family is returned to mundane reality "in the broccoli patch" (183).

L'Engle articulates hope, in this novel as in the other two, by emphasising the spiritual power of love between human beings. Although in each instance the young people are assisted by supernatural agencies—angels in the first novel, a cherubim who looks "like a drive of deformed dragons" in the second (117) and by a unicorn named Gaudior in the third, in each case it is the strong force of human love which wins through.

The second novel in the trilogy is *A Wind in the Door* and this time Charles Wallace is in danger of death from a disease in the mitochondria of his bloodstream. The cancerous cells are analogised with human self-aggrandisement in an episode where Meg, her schoolteacher, Mr. Jenkins, and Proginoskes, the cherubim are inside Charles Wallace's body, inside the mitochondrion itself:

Mr. Jenkins asked [Meg], 'Why did Hitler want to control the world? Or Napoleon? Or Tiberius?'

'I don't know. I don't know why anyone would. I think it would be awful.'

'But you admit they did, Margaret?'

'They wanted to,' she conceded. 'But they didn't succeed.'

'They did a remarkably good job of succeeding for a period of time, and they will not lightly be forgotten. A great many people perished during the years of their rules.'

'But farandolae—why would little farandolae like Sporos—'

'They appear to be not that unlike human beings.' (178)

Charles Wallace is saved, but only at great cost to the cherubim, who has "Xed"—un-named—himself, and his fate is uncertain, although it is clear that the powers of evil have not taken control of him. The happy ending is subverted by the cost of the enterprise, and Meg adds that the element of sadness is the price humans pay for human affection:

'I wish human beings couldn't have feelings. I am having feelings. They hurt.' (200)

Meg is right, of course; there is a price to pay for being human, for possessing even the love which reaches out to "save" other human beings. This is a fantasy, and the journey through Charles Wallace's bloodstream merely appropriates a familiar plot. But L'Engle gives her characters real humanity, sets them in a fallible, unusual family, subjects them to the stares of schoolfellows and the community, and makes them suffer the consequences of loving one another. In love there is hope; but in love there is pain. For that matter, when hope is strongest, pain also is often at its strongest. Pain seems sometimes even to generate hope; in hope lies the strength to endure pain.

In the third book of the trilogy, Meg is married to Calvin, the boy she has befriended all along. Calvin's mother is a reclusive, embittered woman, older than her years, a woman who is difficult to love and whose presence is often taciturn and disruptive. She is described at a Thanksgiving dinner held by Meg's parents:

> Meg's mother-in-law was...silent, but that was not surprising. What was surprising was that she had agreed to come to them for Thanksgiving dinner. Mrs. O'Keefe must have been no more than a few years older than Mrs. Murry, but she looked like an old woman. She had lost most of her teeth, and her hair was yellowish and unkempt, and looked as if it had been cut with a blunt knife. Her habitual expression was one of resentment. Life had not been kind to her, and she was angry with the world, especially with the Murrys...(11)

But Mrs. O'Keefe is rather more than she seems. When Meg's father breaks the news of an impending war with a small South American state led by a crazed dictator called Mad Dog Branzillo, Mrs. O'Keefe offers a rune, a few lines of verse, in which she says there is great power. In order to avert the war, Charles Wallace travels space and time with the unicorn Gaudior—a symbol for Christ, not merely in identification of unicorns with Christ in medieval belief, but also because of his name, which in Latin means "joy." And at various stages in history, Charles Wallace and the unicorn influence the choices made by Mad Dog Branzillo's ancestors, so that the man who was nicknamed "El Rabioso" has become "El Zarco," the Blue-Eyed. "El Rabioso was never born," Charles Wallace tells Meg (254).

In the course of his adventures, Charles Wallace enters the bodies of some of the characters, and in this there is great danger. Drained of his physical and spiritual strength, he returns to the mundane world near death. It is Mrs. O'Keefe who utters the rune:

> I place all Heaven with its power
> And the sun with its brightness
> And the snow with its whiteness

And the fire with all the strength it hath
And the lightning with its rapid wrath,
And the winds with their swiftness along their path,
And the sea with its deepness,
And the rocks with their steepness,
And the earth with its starkness,
All these I place
By God's almighty help and grace
Between myself and the powers of darkness! (247-48)

In this ending, too, there is pain. Mrs. O'Keefe has truly given herself for Charles Wallace. She lies dying at the end of the novel, knowing that she will never see the grandchild Meg is expecting. And Meg "has feelings" again, feelings of pain and frustration: "There's so much more to her than meets the eye. I hate the thought of losing her, just as we're discovering her" (256). The family has never until now tried to discover what Mrs. O'Keefe's story is; in this failure lies the scepticism of this novel. The fact of belief is never enough; it must be accompanied by the actualising of love. Mrs. O'Keefe achieves this; the family for whom she has given her life can only regret and wonder. These books have profound messages for their young readers, and much of their value lies in depicting the difficulties of life being overcome through human love. The supernatural adventures draw the readers in to fantastical worlds, but these are worlds at which the readers themselves can marvel— astronomy, medical science and intuition. Most of all, there is the strong hope that in moments of dire need, there will be someone who cares enough to do as Mrs. O'Keefe has done; as Charles Wallace reminds Meg, "In this fateful hour, it was herself she placed between us and the powers of darkness" (256). And as the scriptures have it, this is the greatest love of all.

Less obviously religious, but with similar messages of scepticism and hope, are the five books in Susan Cooper's sequence, *The Dark is Rising*. From the very title of the sequence, also the title of one of the novels within it, there is an intimation of ongoing evil, against which the efforts of humanity, those on the side of good, seem frustratingly futile.

The sequence combines two separate stories. The first involves children named Jane, Barney and Simon who come in the first novel to holiday in Cornwall with their mysterious Great-Uncle Merriman Lyons. They uncover a mystery map, which leads them to an ancient grail or chalice. In the pursuit of this treasure, the children are thwarted and threatened by a quartet of evil people who turn out to have more than human powers. There is also, they discover, something more than human about their "Gumerry," and the books which follow explore their adventures under his guiding hands.

The second story concerns Will, the seventh son of a seventh son, and therefore the possessor of special powers. He joins Merriman in a fight against the Dark, the forces of evil. It is a deeply sceptical book, in which Will travels through time and space to prevent the Dark from possessing the land. He is in a church service, celebrating Christmas— a time when one might be forgiven for assuming all would be well in the spiritual realm. But even in the role of choirboy in his church, Will feels the presence of Dark about him:

Noise broke suddenly into Will's mind, a shrieking and dreadful howling in the place of the familiar cadences. He had heard it before. It was the sound of the besieging Dark, which he had heard outside the Manor Hall where he had sat with Merriman and the Lady, in some century unknown. But in a church? said Will the Anglican choirboy, incredulous: surely you can't feel it inside a church? Ah, said Will the Old One unhappily, any church of any religion is vulnerable to their attack, for places like this are where men give thought to matters of the Light and the Dark. He hunched his head down between his shoulders as the noise beat at him—and then it vanished again, as the Rector's voice was ringing out alone. (156)

The stories of Will and of Barney, Simon and Jane entwine, and through them all there is the intimation of some greater battle looming ahead. In the final book of the sequence, *Silver on the Tree*, Cooper carefully brings together all the elements she has carefully developed in the previous four stories. In the mystical land of Wales, there is a battle between the Dark and the Light for the crystal sword, the final instrument by which the Light might be, at least for the present, victorious. Another Old One, the Welsh boy Bran, gives up the offer of immortality as Merriman—now revealed in this modern-day Arthuriad as Merlin—tells him that the bonds of love are stronger even than those of High Magic (278). Bran's decision to remain with those mortals who love him is the right thing, not merely for the boy, but also, as Merriman tells him, "for the world" (280). But the ending is not altogether optimistic. The Dark may have been overcome in this instance, but Merriman leaves the children with a warning:

'For remember,' he said, 'that it is altogether your world now. You and all the rest. We have delivered you from evil, but the evil that is inside men is at the last a matter for men to control. The responsibility and the hope and the promise are in your hands— your hands and the hands of children of all men on this earth. The future cannot blame the present, just as the present cannot blame the past. The hope is always here, always alive, but only your fierce caring can fan it into a fire to warm the world.' (282)

Hope, then, lies in the caring and commitment of the world's children to "work and care and [remain] watchful" so that "the worse will never, ever, triumph over the better." The children make a promise: "We'll try... We'll try our best." Merriman assures them that "Nobody can promise more than that" (283).

Cooper allows the intrusion of myth and magic into the fictionalised mundane world, and like Lewis, resurrects Logres, the spiritual Britain of the legendary King Arthur, to influence matters in the present day. Her sequence is sceptical of traditional religion, but she articulates hope in and through the caring and commitment of human beings. In emphasising the power of love, greater even than the "High Magic," Cooper is not far from L'Engle in offering hope for the future.

Lucy Boston's *Green Knowe* stories follow the same pattern as Cooper's, in the intermingling of times and place, so that the old house at Green Knowe is "haunted" by ghosts from the past who are actualised in the sharing of adventures with Tolly, the grandson of the owner of the house, Mrs. Oldknow. Tolly also ventures into the past; but in most cases the adventures have no sense of menace of threat. In contrast with the rest, however, the final book in the series, *An Enemy at Green Knowe,* introduces the concepts of witchcraft and demonology, and the visitor to Green Knowe, Melanie D. Powers, is almost a female Faustus figure, selling her soul and personality to the powers of darkness.

The defeat of Melanie's evil powers is effected, not through the power of a religious exorcism, but through the absent-minded discovery of an Invocation by a scholarly boarder in a cottage on the property near the house, Mr. Pope, and by an incantation chanted by the two boys, Tolly and his Chinese friend, Ping. As a result of their combined efforts, Melanie's demon lord forsakes her, leaving her "An empty, powerless woman, crumpled up and distracted" (138). Although after the episode, Melanie Powers leaves Green Knowe, and the fathers of the two boys arrive amid much jubilation, Boston offers no real assurance that the powers of darkness will not arise again, nor does she offer much hope except the simple "happy ending" she devises in the return of the parents. The Green Knowe books have a degree of popularity, but in contrast with those of L'Engle and Cooper, their tales are slight, offering neither a cogent scepticism nor an enlivening hope beyond the immediate need for some kind of resolution to her tales.

The works of Alan Garner are almost *sui generis*, although they, too, combine the potency of a sense of place with the deep power of myth. Natalie Prior has noted that for Garner, myth is essentially an operation of the intellect, a new way of looking at and understanding the world through the combination of myth and landscape (18). As Garner himself remarked, his fantasies have become more and more "engaged with human personality," and "more internal and less objective" (Garner 23). Two of his children's novels which are intensely sceptical and indeed troublesome because of their violence are *The Owl Service* and *Elidor.* Elidor is a dismal world where "wounds do not heal" (31). It is a world which has been overtaken by darkness, and the evil which has beset Elidor is "leaking," as it were, back to the "real" world of Manchester. There is deep scepticism in the history of Elidor's decline. As Malebron, a resident of Elidor, tells the boy Roland,

> The darkness grew...It is always there. We did not watch, and the power of night closed on Elidor. We had so much of ease that we did not mark the signs—a crop blighted, a spring failed, a man killed. Then it was too late—war, and seige, and betrayal, and the dying of the light. (32)

This warning—to be watchful, lest the powers of the Dark arise—is very similar to that in Cooper's novels. But here the Dark encroaches also on the real world, on Roland's own house, threatening his family. The door to his house becomes a door to Elidor, and as it comes under attack, Roland pours himself out: "...after that there was nothing: and into this nothing the porch began to fall" (106).

Later, at a Christmas celebration, Roland and the children he is visiting with his family begin to play with a planchette, which had belonged to their hostess's mother who had been a Spiritualist. They receive a message from Malebron of Elidor, and a drawing of a unicorn appears on the piece of paper upon which they are drawing. Shortly afterwards, when they are outdoors, a unicorn manifests itself near them, fierce and furious, leaving them startled and afraid.

Elidor is a Waste Land (though Garner spells it Wasteland) which needs the unicorn's song to heal it. But the unicorn is trapped in the mundane world. In an instant when the two worlds are almost merged, men arrive from Elidor attempting to kill the unicorn to prevent him from singing. Wounded, the unicorn goes berserk, and rushes about, and is finally fatally speared by one of the men. But not before the children have encouraged him to sing, and the world of Elidor has been restored, no longer a Waste Land, but a place where "Streams danced and rivers were set free, and all the shining air was new" (159). But though the song of the dying unicorn goes on, "a note of beauty and terror," it is not enough; the children must send back the "treasures" they found in the old slum, treasures from Elidor—a stone, a spear, a cup and a cauldron. Elidor is healed, and it is no longer a danger to the mundane world. But the children are left in a slum, and there is no benefit to the real world from this encounter with the mythic dimensions of Elidor. The book is full of violence and terror, and there seems to be no real articulation of hope, except that it is possible to restore myth to the realm of myth, so that it does not intrude upon the real world. The world of myth is a world of wonder; so much Garner concedes as we glimpse the healed Elidor; but it is also a threatening world, cruel and menacing, when it crosses the boundaries of time and space and invades the real world.

The Owl Service is constructed around the same kind of thesis; the mythic world of the past intrudes into present, this time through the dinner service with the design of an owl upon the places, and paper cut-out owls with which the children are playing. Fear and terror build up as Alison, the daughter of the owner of the house where the children are staying, feels increasingly as though she will burst: "My body gets tighter and tighter and—and then it's as if my skin's suddenly holes like that chicken wire, and it all shoots out" (67). Only old Huw Halfbacon, who works in the garden, is able to warn them about the power of the myth which haunts the place. The myth involves the lady Blodeuwedd, who betrayed her husband, Lleu, with her lover, Gronw Pebyr. The myth comes, of course, from *The Mabinogion*; the fresh but frightening touch which Garner gives it is to actualise it in the present place and time. The characters of the myth relive their suffering through the humans who dwell in the place where the mythic events occurred; as old Huw tells the children, "Lleu, Blodeuwedd and Gronw Pebyr. They are the three who suffer every time, for in them the power of this valley is contained, and through them the power is loosed" (72). Huw also warns the children that through their imagining of the shapes on the service of plates and in their cutting-out owls, they awaken the mythic characters to replay their ancient sufferings.

In the final episode, Alison is possessed by the entity of Blodeuwedd; but Roger realises the need to transform the owls into flowers. With his encouragement, she reconstructs the images as flowers, and the mythic presence leaves her as petals fall about them from the skylight and the rafters (156). This is a book which also dwells fatalistically on the replaying of a myth through human characters, a replaying which involves also the experience of mythic pain and suffering. The only hope which is articulated is that achieved through the realisation that the lady wanted to be flowers and not owls; a realisation available to the children early in the novel, thanks to the advice of Huw, the old gardener. But there is real terror in the physical effects of the mythic replaying on Alison, and the lifting of the mythic presence at the end is too abrupt to offer a satisfactory resolution to the plot. It is hardly closure; there is no sense of completion, and the emotionally charged atmosphere of the last few pages remains disturbingly with the reader. Neither *Elidor* nor *The Owl Service* offers what Tolkien calls "Consolation"; the element of Escape into the mythic world is charged with terror, and the return to mundane reality is inconclusive and unsatisfactory. These are, perhaps, the most sceptical of the children's books to emerge in the late sixties and early seventies, for unlike most other fantasies there is little to hope for, no real positive gain, only a lifting of horror, and that without any real hope of permanency. For Garner's myths, played out again and again, threaten recurrence. He seems to have no conception of "good myth," myth which is imbued with truth and which brings with it imaginative wholeness and healing.

Patricia Wrightson uses the same kind of mythic device in her Australian fantasies, but her lively spiritual creatures are drawn from Aboriginal legends and the ancient Dreamtime of which they tell. Although her creatures are mischievous, and often annoying to her human characters, they are not intrinsically evil, and readerly sympathy is directed to them, and to the Dreamtime which is their origin.

In *A Little Fear*, Mrs. Tucker, a determined elderly lady, plans her escape from the Sunset Nursing Home—a place which, in its own way, offers a kind of patronising totalitarian rule after the style of Ken Kesey's asylum in *One Flew Over the Cuckoo's Nest*:

> When you were old, she knew, you really were a sort of child. When the things you used to do were all done, and your body and your mind grew slower, other people took over. They called your dear, or Agnes, just as if you were a child, and kept you in a clean bright nursery, and brought you warm underclothes that you didn't want. They were worried and looked after you until, if you weren't careful, you were a prisoner of their care. Just like a child. (6)

This is a gentle totalitarianism, and one that is obviously well-intentioned, but the end result is the same as in Orwell's *Nineteen Eighty-Four* or Lewis's *That Hideous Strength*—dehumanisation. Mrs. Tucker has an avenue of escape, however, and despite her slowing mind has the wit to avail herself of it. She uses a legitimate holiday to find herself a cottage on a disused farm property which has come to her from her brother. And there she proves herself to be extremely resourceful, first buying a dog for company and some kind of protection, and then adapting herself to new surroundings, and even managing to row herself a little way across the Broad, the flooded valley which her cottage overlooks.

Mrs. Tucker's new existence is troubled, however, by a series of events which rather resemble the Old Testament plagues—with visitations of rats, frogs, and winged insects, all designed to make her leave the property. The perpetrator of these pranks—for pranks they are, and not intrinsically evil—is an ancient spirit, the Njimbin, who has taken up residence in the deserted fowl run—a haven Mrs. Tucker appropriates once she decides to keep hens:

> From the fowlyard, the old eyes of the Njimbin watched her go: strong in spirit, peaceful in mind, slow in legs and stiff in back. The Njimbin knew old women. It also knew dogs: hunters too big for a Njimbin's spear and too close to man to be led or managed by a Njimbin...In its long time on the ridges above the Broad, the Njimbin had come to know old women and dogs; but it lived only for now and never drew on the past to plan for the future. A sly and tricky spirit, quick to seize the chance of the moment, but not wise. It only watched...(20)

Mrs. Tucker endures the cheeky torments of the Njimbin bravely, but is ready to move, at her daughter's suggestion, into town, selling the property on the Broad, but retaining her independence, courageous enough to face "another problem still to come, life to be lived in your own way without other people doing it for you" (109). The Njimbin has "won" temporarily (the new owners of the property might well overcome it); but Mrs. Tucker has also "won" her battle for independence and respect. Wrightson handles the aspect of the European facing age-old Dreamtime spirits very well, eliciting readerly sympathy for both, and leading young readers in particular to an appreciation of the realities underlying Aboriginal legends.

When Wrightson allows the Dreamtime entities to be threatening and fearsome, she does so against the European tradition, showing quite clearly that Europeans are still to a large degree aliens in the ancient land of Australia. In *The Nargun and the Stars*, an ancient rock begins to move, and with its movement across time and space it brings fear and dread. Nevertheless, Wrightson's sympathies are directed to the ancient entity: it is not evil, merely, as with most ancient entities in the invaded continent, bewildered, displaced, dismayed by the new order:

Sometimes [the Nargun] remembered the world's making and cried for that long agony. Sometimes it felt anger: for a fallen tree, a dried-up pool, an intruder, or for hunger. Then too it cried. It had a sort of love: a response to the deep, slow rhythms of the earth; and when it felt the earth's crust swell to the pull of the moon it sometimes called in ecstasy. It had no fear; but a wide sunny place, or any strange thing, made it uneasy. Then it crouched in stony stillness...(10)

The Nargun arrives in Wongadilla, in the Hunter Valley (near Newcastle, New South Wales), and Simon Brent encounters it, and with it the terror of the unknown. With the help of other ancient spirits, Simon at least brings it to a kind of rest, at least for the time being. And even Simon, at the end of his terror and in the generosity of relief, is able to say of it, *"Poor thing..."* (158). Wrightson brings the ancient myths to life and has them impinge upon daily existence, but in doing so she maintains the integrity of the myth, refusing to see them as evil, and using them to create understanding between the people of the Dreamtime and the Europeans who have made the oldest continent their home. This is a technique opposite to that of Garner, who sees myth intruding violently upon modern existence. Wrightson attempts a syncretism between the ancient and the modern, and for the most part she is successful.

The book in which she shows the ancient creatures working towards the same ends as present-day children is her *An Older Kind of Magic*. The plot of this book is one with which readers in any westernised country can identify. Parking spaces are at a premium in Sydney, so a developer wants to resume part of the Botanical Gardens to build a huge car park.

The three children who live in the city—their parents are caretakers respectively of an office block and of a shop—are Rupert and Selina Potter, and their friend Benny Golightly. The gardens are their playground, and their allegiance is very much to the expanse of greenery and water which is their second home.

To Sir Mortimer Wyvern, however, the city "gets its living from Commerce," and Commerce must have car parks. The Botanical Gardens to him are merely "fifty acres of sentimental waste" (10). He reckons without the children, however, who relish demonstrations they see taking place regularly about them, "The people marching with banners that they would never let you read, looking excited and important as they marched" (32). Sir Mortimer reckons without the world-weary Ernest Hawke, advertising man, and without the Nyol, the Net-Net, the Bitarr and the Pot-Koorok, ancient spirits who dwell in the gardens and who return to the upper regions in time to work their magic on Sir Mortimer, who is turned to stone, and remains in the Gardens, a self-important statue of himself.

Together with the emergence of the ancient creatures from under the earth, there is also the effect of a comet passing close in the heavens which temporarily gives the amateur magician, Ernest Hawke, surprising powers. With the children's help, he organises a demonstration, consisting of shop dummies who come magically to life and who carry advertising signs, which disturbs the high-level meeting in the Government building on the top of which Rupert and Selina live. The demonstration achieves its aims, and the plans for the car park are abandoned. There is a wry commentary upon Commerce as the "statue" of Sir Mortimer becomes a favourite plaything of the ancient spirits:

> Sir Mortimer had never been so loved.
> For stone is stone; and men whose drills break into the living stone should take care. They may find what they do not expect. (149)

Wrightson's scepticism is concerned with the place of "elves and dragons and unicorns" in Australia; she writes, "They have never belonged here, and no ingenuity can make them real" (150). She is, however, as ardent a "believer" in magic as American and English fantasists:

> ...magic has still a real and important place in our stories—most real when the magic is dark, mysterious, and a little frightening, as it always was. And magic must be real in place, as well as in kind, for men were never stupidly gullible. The spirits they saw at the edge of their vision were shaped by something real: by the swirling of the snow, or the darkness of a pool, or the terror of a mountain. (150)

Wrightson's vision captures imaginatively and sympathetically the spirit of Australia's ancient mythic legacy. She manages to imbue in the mischief of her Dreamtime spirits a moral point, that human beings have a responsibility to the land to treat it as a living entity. Towards commerce and "development," Wrightson has (and engenders in her readers) a healthy scepticism. She arouses hope for a new vision of Australia—and indeed for any country for which land has a mythical value—in the moral messages available to us in ancient myth.

Children's fantasies of the kind discussed in this chapter—and there are many more of value than there is space to treat—draw upon what G.K. Chesterton calls "the ethics of Elfland" (*Orthodoxy* 86) to allow scepticism of a kind in order to rehabilitate new hope for the future, a new understanding of the elements of fantasy and myth which alert us to the truth about our world and our place in it. We are, despite our tendency to self-aggrandisement, merely "little people" in a vast cosmos, and yet even little people can bring about great good when they understand the nature of truth. In conveying mythic truth, the writers of juvenile fantasy are performing the roles of moral guides and teachers, appropriating, as adult fantasists do also, the role of priest and prophet. As C.S. Lewis observed a generation ago, traditional religion is the poorer for its lack of enchantment and visionary imagination, and responses to it are paralysed by the implicit demands it makes for suitably reverential attitudes. Lewis had battled with this experience in his own youth. He writes,

> The whole subject was associated with lowered voices; almost as if it were something medical. But supposing that by casting all these things into an imaginary world, stripping them of their stained glass and Sunday school associations, one could make them for the first time appear in their real potency? Could one not thus steal past those watchful dragons? I thought one could. (73)

Though Lewis's Narnian stories are more overtly "Christian" than most of the children's fantasies available today, there is no doubt that other authors have captured for themselves something of Lewis's vision. And indeed, there seems to be a realisation from theologians that something of the imaginative vision of the feeling intellect available in fantasy writing is required for a rebirth of spirituality in this age (Kelly *passim*). If there is a flowback of imaginative and mythic elements into traditional religion, it will owe much to the Romantic vision so carefully preserved in this age by the writers of Fantasy.

Chapter Eleven:
In the Paths of the Prophets:
Some Recent Trends in Fantasy Literature

...your sons and daughters will prophesy,
Your old men will dream dreams,
Your young men will see visions...

And I will display wonders in the sky and
on the earth.
Joel II: xxviii-xxx

As the twentieth century draws to a close, fantasy literature continues to proliferate. A glance at forthcoming publication lists of the best-known companies reveals that volumes are being produced, as Vonnegut suggests, "at top speed." These publications are clearly a response to a perceived public demand, and the courses which are also now available at colleges and universities throughout the world also indicate that to some extent, the genre has gained not only academic respectability, but also serious critical attention.

The sheer numbers of new books now being issued prevents any exhaustive analytic attempt to define the directions fantasy is taking. But in the 1990s, Tolkien's publishers are reissuing a number of his works—including *The Lord of the Rings* and *The Hobbit*—and C.S. Lewis and Ursula Le Guin also remain in print. This evidence suggests that writers and readers of Fantasy still recognize the influence and importance of the "masters" of the art, and that the traditions established by them are being maintained. As well, it is apparent that there is also a great demand for the "sword and sorcery" kind of Fantasy that this study has not attempted to treat; usually issued only in paperback, these are usually highly formulaic and deal with political situations or the stuff of murder mysteries or thrillers in which only the locations are changed, and those mostly by giving them improbable names. To Tolkien, the philologist, and to Lewis, philosopher, philologist and literary critic, names were important, part of an entire linguistic system, and therefore needed to be consistent with the wider language of the fantastical peoples to whom they were applied. In less well-researched works, some of the names look as though they are the result of a lucky-dip in a bowl of alphabet soup, featuring strange configurations of consonants, usually with a great many z's and j's. C.S. Lewis once remarked that even when parallel universes or fantastical worlds were used, they should not be merely the setting for a tale which could be set as well in London or New York: the setting must be a logical, emotional and atmospheric part of the plot and characterisation (Filmer 53). Some of the most recent fantasies which, although original in every way, maintain the tradition established by Tolkien, Lewis and Le Guin are those which consciously avail themselves of the power of myth and magic aroused by a pervading spirit of place. Among the more serious recent works of fantasy which evoke a sense of place are Marion Zimmer Bradley's *The Mists of Avalon*, Laura Gilmour Bennett's *A Wheel of Stars*, Lindsay Clarke's *The Chymical Wedding*, and Tom Robbins's *Skinny Legs and All*. These works are also profoundly sceptical of established religion, but they offer, through the revival of ancient nature myths, a clear articulation of hope.

Martin Hocke's *The Ancient Solitary Reign* is less concerned with place than with the notion of using "little creatures" as a metaphor for humanity: he chooses a society of owls, and his choice, although it allows him to raise social and political issues, also raises very real difficulties with the suspension of disbelief. It, too, is a profoundly sceptical novel—sceptical of all the belief systems of a destructive humanity. All four novels, however, "speak" religion of various kinds, activating in the present age a new-age Romanticism, the mysticism of which owes as much to Blake[1] as to Coleridge, but which nevertheless continues to articulate both prophetic warnings and priestly consolation to the readers of the late twentieth century—readers who, more than in any other age, have the greatest need for them.

Marion Bradley's *The Mists of Avalon* is unique among twentieth century versions of the Arthuriad because of its feminist focus and sympathetic treatment of Igraine, Morgause, Morgaine and Viviane, the Lady of the Lake. The Christian religion is depicted as cold and comfortless—or in Blakean terms, Urizenic—and is debunked in favour of the worship of the pagan Goddess whom Viviane is driven to invoke:

> Goddess, do not take the power from me, not yet, not for a little while. Mother, you know I do not ask it for myself, only that this land may be safe until I can place it into the hands which I have prepared to safeguard it. (195)

The narrative is rich in magic and mystery, hinting at some of the secrets of Hermeticism (through the power of Merlin the Magician to perform the Great Marriage), and describing some of the Druidic rites which pervade the Britain to which the Romans bring Christianity. There is a very great tension between the new religion and the old. While Guinevere (Called Gwenhwyfar in the book) is a Christian who seeks to convert her husband, Arthur, her life is tormented by guilt. She is unable to come to terms with her own sexuality and passion. Preparing to make love with Lancelet, she rehearses her guilt for what she perceives to be a sin:

God will punish Camelot for that sin, she thought suddenly. For Arthur's sin and for mine...and Lancelet's...(839)

The book, then, is highly sceptical of the claims and consolations of the Christian religion, but affirms hope through the individuation offered to women by the Goddess: "They are the Goddess. And I am the Goddess. And there is no other" (803), and in the appropriation by the Christian women of the worship of the Mother Goddess through images of the Virgin Mary and other female saints. "God is so great and terrible I am always afraid before *his* altar, but here in the Chapel of Mary, we...may come to her as our Mother, too..." says a young girl showing Morgaine the Christian chapel (875). At the sight of a statue of St. Brigid, Morgaine bows her head, recognising "the Goddess as she is worshipped in Ireland." It is in this chapel, where Christianity and paganism meet, that Morgaine utters with great faith and hope, "The Goddess is within us, yes, but now I know that you are in the world too, now and always, just as you are in Avalon and in the hearts of all men and women..." (876). The Goddess of the novel is quite clearly the nature Goddess representing the creative power of nature, especially of the feminine. Although Christianity is debunked, it is rehabilitated somewhat in these closing paragraphs for the way it unwittingly fosters the rituals and worship of the Great Mother. As in Russell Hoban's *Riddley Walker*, there is comfort and hope in the religion of the Mother Goddess "who has her woom in Cambry;" Hoban, like Bradley, succeeds in "marrying" an unsuspecting Christianity (through the shape of the sanctuary of Canterbury Cathedral) to the pagan religion of his Moon Goddess, who is clearly drawn from the same archetype as Bradley's Mother Goddess.

The same subversion of the Christian religion appears in Lindsay Clarke's *The Chymical Wedding* (1989) which tells two parallel tales of the quest to achieve the Chymical Wedding between male and female, spirit and matter. In the mid-nineteenth century, a country rector in East Anglia, Edwin Frere, brings his wife Emilia to a small village where they are welcomed by the local squire, Henry Agnew, and his daughter Louisa. A strange relationship begins between Louisa and Edwin, as Louisa attempts to finish the task her father cannot—a written record of the Hermetic mysteries. More than one hundred and thirty years later, a newly-separated husband, Alex Darken, takes refuge in the same village, and meets the ageing poet, Edward Nesbit, and his lover, the young

American woman, Laura; they too are attempting the Chymical Wedding, having discovered fragments of the notes made by Louisa long ago.

Like the ladies of Avalon, Louisa finds comfort in the worship of the Goddess. She tries to explain to the bewildered Frere the mystery of the Mother Goddess:

> I know how terrible she appears. I know how to the uninitiated eye she seems to offer only immolation, dismemberment, the dark. But that is only the face of her own hurt. She has other faces, Edwin. She is our Mother. She is our Mother and her other face is love. And she will not be denied because she too is truth...Hers is the peace which passeth understanding. It was hers long before the Christian Church claimed it for its own...(392)

Edwin sees in Louisa at that moment "No priest but priestess, her face vivid with the living presence of the goddess for whom she pleaded now" (393). Edward and Laura are dabbling in the same mysteries, enchanted by the spirit of place, the mystical power of the cottage where Louisa had worked on her Hermetic text. Drawn into the oddly magnetic relationship between the poet and the young woman, partly because of his attraction to and sexual desire for Laura, Alex discovers what the Chymical Wedding might mean to the world:

> [There was a force] threatening to blow up in the alchemist's face unless those warring tensions could be reconciled. So that was it—people who quaked were alembicks...They were members of the chymical wedding.

> With that realization I saw how the whole dream was elegantly structured around the tension of opposing forces: male, female; capitalist, communist; secular, spiritual; Catholic, Protestant; hierarchy, equality. It was a dream about conflict and reconciliation, of fission and fusion. (415)

Clearly, Clarke is addressing the same concerns as both Bradley and Hoban—the notion of divisions between human beings, divisions which result in conflict and war, disharmony and hatred. It is clear, too, that like the other two authors, Clarke is deeply sceptical of the role of the Christian church in bringing about these divisions, and he stresses the unity to be achieved by the Chymical Wedding if its mystery can be solved. Laura and Edward do not succeed in their attempt to achieve it; but the book ends on a note of hope expressed through Edward's dream of the alchemical palace beyond death (534) and Alex's concluding assurance that "once you begin to admit the truth there is no ending" (539).

A similar blend of mysticism and magic pervades much of the most recent fantasy. The rejection of traditional Christianity and the focus on the Great Mother Divinity seems to suggest a disillusionment with the patriarchal hierarchy of Christianity and the lack of compassion in much orthodox church dogma. The authors seem to express, on behalf of their readers, the need for a religion which offers a sense of nurturing from a god of compassion and comfort, and the achievement of self-actualisation through unity with this maternal presence which is perceived in and through all nature. It can be argued, and sermons from Christian pulpits do indeed argue, that all these reassuring elements are available in Christianity. And yet, often, the Christian rituals seem empty, as though Christians themselves go through the motions despite or their own intrinsic, though unadmitted, scepticism.

A very recent book which exemplifies all these points is Tom Robbins's *Skinny Legs and All*. This has not been classified as fantasy; it is aimed at the general fiction market, but it is the element of fantasy which gives this book especial appeal.

It tells two stories which intersect at various key points. The first is the love story of Ellen Cherry Charles and Boomer Petway, who set off on their honeymoon in a caravan which Boomer, by virtue of his skill at welding, has turned into a giant mobile turkey. They enjoy a few moments of vigorous sexual congress in a cave and awaken two mystical objects—a conch shell and a painted stick—which were used in the worship of the Great Mother Goddess, Astarte, in pre-Biblical times.

In fact, according to the history lesson these objects give to the can of pork and beans, the dirty sock and the silver spoon left behind by the human lovers who flee from the mysterious movements of the stick and the shell, the Bible is in fact the story of the displacement of the Female Goddess by the patriarchally approved male Deity, Yahweh.

Robbins explains:

Who was Astarte? She was a goddess; rather, she was the Goddess, the Great Mother, the Light of the World, the most ancient and widely revered divinity in human history. Shrines to her date back to the Neolithic Period, and there was not one Indo-European culture that failed to remove with its kiss the mud from her sidereal slippers. In comparison, 'God,' as we moderns call Yahweh (often misspelled 'Jehovah') was a Yahnny-come-lately who would never approach her enormous popularity. She was the mother of God, as indeed, she was the mother of all. As beloved as she was for her life-giving and nurturing qualities, the only activities of hers acceptable to the patriarchs, she was mistress over destruction as well as creation, representing, according to one scholar, 'the abyss that is the source and the end, the ground of all being.' (44)

The focus of the novel is the continually festering wound of division and racial hatred in the Middle East, and although the novel is set in America, the concerns of the Middle East, the womb, indeed as Robbins suggests at the end, the vagina of the world, are in constant focus. The motley collection of objects—spoon, shell, stick, sock and can of beans—

set off on a pilgrimage to Jerusalem to pay homage to the Great Mother, in whose honour the Third Temple is to be built.

Although they are inanimate, these objects can speed up the movements of their molecules to accomplish many marvellous things—locomotion, starting a fire, welding the can of beans together after it was split open, and (except for the sock) their arrival in Jerusalem. At various times they encounter Ellen Cherry Charles, left alone in New York when Boomer gets instant acclaim for his "art" (thanks to the turkey-trailer) and is commissioned to make a huge public sculpture in Jerusalem. Ellen, on the other hand, is drawn to the imperceptible movements of Turn Around Norman, a pavement performer, and spends much of her time avoiding a fundamentalist preacher from her mid-west home town. The Reverend Buddy Winkler is involved in a Zionist/Fundamentalist Christian plot to hasten the Apocalypse and Armageddon, and his portrayal as a pock-marked and boil-ridden, saxophone-voiced, hypnotic speaker with extreme views and unusual sexual proclivities serves as a scathing commentary on the Christian religion.

The climax of the book—a fitting term for a novel which is in many ways a celebration of sexuality—comes when a nubile sixteen-year-old belly dancer undertakes to perform the Dance of the Seven Veils in the restaurant operated by Ellen's employers, Abu the Arab and Spike the Jew (the restaurant is called "Isaac and Ishmael's" and attracts a number of bomb threats and one or two bombs as well). During the dance, those who watch it (the ratio between males and females in the audience is 2:1) receive all manner of intuitional enlightenment, including the information that religion as understood in Western societies is repressive and static, while the Divine principle is free and fluid.

As the dance draws to a close, Winkler, deprived of his trip to Jerusalem to destroy the Dome of the Rock by an astute Vice-President and the intervention of the CIA, comes to the restaurant spoiling for trouble. He is shot by a police officer who has been watching the dance; and the police officer and the dancer are themselves shot. Their wounds, unlike Winkler's, are not fatal. The violence in the restaurant is a metonym for the violence which has long dogged the Middle East, arising from one man's dreams of self-aggrandisement (If the Messiah doesn't come, he says, "Then I reckon I'll have to step in and be the Messiah" [390]). And to this are added misunderstandings and ill-considered actions.

There is a conventionally "happy ending"; Boomer and Ellen are reunited, and have achieved a measure of respect for and understanding of one another. But the reader is very conscious of the open-endedness of the wider plot, of the lack of political resolution. After all, until all the world experiences the revelations permitted to those who watch the

Salome's Dance of the Seven Veils re-enacted in the restaurant, violence and hatred will continue.

And the reader is left with a sense of longing for the restoration of the magic and mystery of the worship of the Goddess, heightened by Ellen Cherry Charles's whispered remark to her visualisation of the departed Turn Around Norman, "Where does magic and beauty go when it's driven from the world?" (417). Into art, Robbins suggests, though not overtly. Ellen herself decides to return to her painting, given up when Boomer's atrocious "talent" overshadowed her more imaginative and delicate work. And then, she decides, "Beauty would just be her everyday thing" (421). The running commentary Robbins offers in this novel *per medium* of the questing stick, shell, sock, spoon and can of beans makes this an intensely polemic work, an apologetic for the ancient religion of the Great Mother, which Robbins sees as the answer for the troubled world of today. In this book, then, the same kinds of questions are asked as in the preceding ones, and the same answer—the reinstatement of the female deity—is offered.

There is a further point to be made about this trend in fantasy to focus on the Great Mother in Nature, and that concerns the notion of "story" itself. Stories traditionally support the parental role, being methods at once of teaching children values and social attitudes and of reassuring them about the structure of the society in which they live. The fable about the boy who cried "Wolf!" is both cautionary and reassuring: help *is* available, but one must only ask for it when it is really needed. Many fairytales are also moral tales in which Good and Evil are portrayed with a heavy saccharine influence on the Good (despite Milton's devil, evil in children's tales is often ugly and frightening). Stories are, in a sense, spells by which parents put their children to sleep, comfort them when they are lonely, and entertain them. They are part of the parental bonding process, and in story there is an intrinsic function of reassurance and nurturing. One might venture that stories are a peculiarly *maternal* function, especially in the era when it was common for mothers to devote their whole time to child-raising. Stories are part of the process of learning to read; they are, in fact, a fundamental part of the whole educational process. But stories come first from parental figures or from those, such as teachers, *in loco parentis*, so that the strong emphasis in these recent works of fantasy upon the maternal might well be an attempt to compensate not only for the departure of the mother figure from the centrality of the family, but also for the discontinuity that this might have caused in the social framework. This not to argue that men do not tell stories to children, or indeed to other adults. Christ's parables and the tales of Hans Christian Andersen, to select two historically remote examples, are evidence that they do. (Nor is this to argue for the socially retrograde step of "returning mothers to the home.")

Nevertheless, in the first instance, stories have traditionally been told by mothers as part of the bonding and socialising process. Are these fantasies alerting late twentieth century society to a fundamental emotional need for parental reassurance? Perhaps. It may well be a later age which will find answers and pass judgment upon late twentieth century Western societies.

In Laura Gilmour Bennett's *A Wheel of Stars*, the same device—of some potent mythic force reaching across the boundaries of time—is used, this time in the pursuit of the Gnostic secrets and the Holy Grail, not in Wales or at Glastonbury, but from the treasure-house of the Cathar heretics of thirteenth century Montségur.

This book also deals with the mingling and blending of episodes which occur in different eras—in this case the love story of Louise Carey and Owen Morgan, and Sancha, a young girl forced to flee from the raid of Knights Templar upon a suspected Cathar village, and Hugo de Franjal, a nobleman sworn to defend his country against the Roman Church and the King of France. The fantasy elements in the book abound as mysterious forces lead Louise and Owen to Montségur; and the antique dealer, Rex Monckton, turns out to be the devil incarnate. The supernatural elements, the blending of history and myth in placing the Holy Grail where historically it was known never to be, in the Cathar treasury (Churton 93-94), and the conflict between good and evil, are all characteristics of fantasy.

Since the religious perspective of this book is Gnostic, the notion of good and evil is rather different from that understood in traditional Christianity. According to Gnostic belief, the world was created by the devil, and humanity must transcend its evil origins through belief in a good God (making one a *Credente*) and by receiving the rite or sacrament of the *Consolamentum*, which liberates the soul from the bonds of the flesh and unites it with the Good. One who has received this rite is one of the *Perfecti* (Churton 69-90). This religious focus seems to stem from both the historical Cathar antipathy towards the medieval Roman church, and perhaps also from the author's disillusionment with and scepticism towards twentieth century Christian orthodoxy. Certainly the religion depicted in this novel has qualities of colour, romance, chivalry and honour which are often lacking from twentieth century Christian experience.

There is, however, some correspondence between the notions of good and evil held by the two authors who collaborated as Laura Gilmour Bennett (Jean Gilmour Harvey and Laura Bennett) and such Christian writers as C.S. Lewis, J.R.R. Tolkien and Madeleine L'Engle. It is the same correspondence as that between Lewis's N.I.C.E. and Orwell's Ingsoc. Evil is associated with power over and control of others, as when

Owen Morgan confronts Rex Monckton in the closing chapters of the novel. Monckton tries to shove Morgan out of his way:

> . . . 'If you're wise, Owen, you'll do as I command.'
>
> 'As you *command?*' The word were a blatant challenge. 'But I'm not wise. If I were wise, I would never have let you steal the Grail from me all those years ago.'
>
> Rex raised an eyebrow and a look of incredulity crossed his face. 'So, you know? How ironic. And all along I thought you were so stupid. But no matter. You're no closer now to having it than you ever were.'
>
> 'And neither are you. It's not meant to belong to you, because you're evil, Rex, and the Grail is wholly good.'
>
> Rex snorted with laughter. 'And you, I suppose, represent goodness. Good, evil— you talk like a schoolboy. There is only one thing that is the measure of any man, my friend, and that is power.' (410-11)

The identification of power with evil, indeed between power and the devil personified, clearly links this novel with those of the Christian fantasists, despite its overt scepticism of traditional Christianity and its focus upon the heretical Cathar sect. There is, it seems, still a place in the late twentieth century for fantasy which defines good and evil, if not as absolutes, then at least in relative terms derived from the notion that it is wrong to exert compulsion over others, either at a personal or at a political level.

Martin Hocke's *The Ancient Solitary Reign* also deals with the same concept of evil, although Hocke tries in this, his first novel, to pack in as many of his political, social and environmental concerns as he can—as if he feels, perhaps, that he will have no other opportunity. The concerns are valid; but in making his novel so heavily polemic, he seems to overlook the need for readers to enjoy the fantasy on its own terms. Nevertheless, one significant aspect of this book is that it attempts to create a credible parallel world in which owls can record their history, sociology and religion and contrast them effectively with those of the human society which they regard with fear and scepticism.

The owls' attitudes are obviously an encoding of the author's own attitudes to the social structures, the religion and the environmental policies of humans. Hocke's polemic is all-too-intrusive for fantasy; or perhaps it follows the models of pre-Glasnost Soviet fantasy, which presents an instructive line.[2] The following passage is an example; Hunter, the Barn Owl, disputes the idea of collective living:

> . . . 'I mean, all crowding together on one tiny patch of land—to our way of thinking, that's positively manlike.'
>
> 'What do you mean by manlike?' Alba asked. 'We have that word as well, but I guess we use it in a different way.'

'Manlike means all swarming together like a mob of mindless peewits,' said Hunter, feeling very knowledgable and clever. 'It means all living on top of one another and getting in each other's way.'

'We have another word for that,' said Alba. 'Gregarious.' It comes from the old language. 'Gregge' means flock and gregarious means wanting to be with others, but it also means getting on with others, too. So it's not an insult in the way your manlike is.'

'But don't you feel diminished?' Hunter asked...

'Oh no,' said Alba, shrugging a little and putting on her wistful look. 'I wouldn't feel at all ashamed to be gregarious. I think it's very sad to be all alone with no one to love and no one to care for you. I think all owls need love and affection at least as much as they need independence. What they need is belonging, commitment and for other owls to care...' (74)

It is clear from this extract that the owls and their society are obvious metaphors for humanity; and certainly the drama which is played out is a very human one; firstly against the devouring Eagle Owl and then against the destruction of the environment. Owl chicks are born deformed and die, thanks to the chemical poisons in the air and also in the food gathered by adult owls. The owls struggle to survive the onslaughts humans make upon nature; and there are always the "firesticks"—the guns of brutal men. The owl hero, Hunter, is killed trying to divert the men's attention from his hen and her chicks as they try to escape the dangerous area. In his dying moments, he manages to be thankful that his death is not agonisingly slow, like those from chemical poisoning, pollution or old age. He sighs for his lost faith and hope, for Alba, the Little Owl who was his first and truest love:

And he died in the belief that they might come together once again in the place where he was going, so far away above the highest mountain and beyond the moon and the stars. His had been a hard life in which he had known sorrow, war and pain but also great happiness and joy, so it was fitting that his last thoughts on earth were of faith and hope for a cleaner future for his species and for himself at long last a deep, eternal peace. (358)

This novel also concludes on a note of hope—perhaps a trifle unconvincingly, given the tragedy of the owl's death. But his death can only be made bearable by the hope that humankind will heed the warning Hocke issues through his device of having owls speak for the other living creatures with whom humans share the planet.

In each of these novels of the nineteen eighties, there is an articulation of hope—hope for the discovery of the Hermetic Mysteries through which the world might be healed, as in *The Chymical Wedding*; hope that we might reconstruct a feminist Camelot in this present age, as in *The Mists of Avalon*; hope that in some way present actions might heal the wounds of the past, and that the power of evil might be overcome, as in *A Wheel of Stars*; and perhaps more prosaically, but nevertheless importantly, the hope that Hocke articulates in his world of the owls, that humans might learn to love and care for one another, for the world they live in, and for the environment they share with all other living creatures.

These are the concerns of the late twentieth century, and the novels represent a necessarily limited selection from the range of hopes and beliefs to which humans are drawn at the close of what has been possibly the most destructive and violent of all centuries—not only because of its wars, but because faith and love have failed, and hope has been perceived to be ebbing. Fantasy, more than ever, performs its priestly, prophetic function, alerting readers to the social and spiritual dangers of apathy and cynicism; while offering reassurance and hope for a better tomorrow. Of all genres, fantasy offers most: healing, a glimpse of the human potential to overcome evil, and strong motivation to fight for the good and to strive for the Grail, whatever we perceive it to be. Perhaps, after all, the scepticism of this century has managed to provoke the writers of fantasy to wear their priestly robes with pride. And if they speak with the voices of prophets, we may hope that they, like Jonah, might end up sulking beneath the juniper tree because their words of warning and of hope have been heard and heeded.

Chapter Twelve:
Fantasy: Imagination, Healing and Hope

There is a curtain, thin as gossamer,
clear as glass, strong as iron, that hangs for ever
between the world of magic and the world that seems
to us to be real. And when once people have found
one of the little weak spots in the curtain which
are marked by magic rings, and amulets, and the
like, almost anything may happen.

E. Nesbit, *The Enchanted Castle* (250)

It is clear that twentieth century fantasy, represented here by the selections from British, American, German and Australian writings in the genre, owes much to the Romantic tradition. The works discussed in this volume are not without flaws; their inclusion has not meant unqualified admiration for them, simply recognition that they appeal to a wide and growing readership. The reason for that appeal is, I believe, that Fantasy offers in this sceptical age what religion would offer in an age of faith—some ways of looking at and explaining the human condition, and of seeing in it something for which to hope. As with Romanticism, Fantasy elevates the human Imagination to a quasi-Divine faculty, able to recreate the elements perceived in the world about us. As with Romanticism, it sees the author in the role of prophet and priest, warning, exhorting and consoling. It speaks, as the Romantics tried to do, in the "real language of men [and women]," meeting them where they are in this century of discontinuity and disillusionment. Fantasy, in this century, has become an important channel for the voices of the visionaries. Whether the visionaries aesthetically uphold some "great literary tradition" is a matter for another study.

What we understand as "Fantasy" has a comparatively recent history. In his seminal work, *Victorian Fantasy*, Stephen Prickett traces the evolution of the word "fantasy" from its earliest origins, when it was often used pejoratively, "implying delusion, hallucination, or simply wishful thinking," as in its use by Longinus, Chaucer and, later, Shakespeare (Prickett 1). The term changed to achieve the meaning it has today in the nineteenth century, largely thanks to the emphasis by the Romantics on the Imagination—especially that of Coleridge, who delighted "in tales of the marvellous and supernatural" (4). In this favourable climate, the collection of fairy stories by the Brothers Grimm and the stories of Hans Andersen both became very popular in the first half of the nineteenth century (Schenkel 275).

Also thanks to the Romantics, with the growing acceptance of Fantasy as a literary *genre* came a special understanding of the role played by the Imagination in the education of children. Indeed, as Elmar Schenkel points out, such authors as Dickens, Ruskin, Thackeray and Southey argued for the "imaginative development of children." The real dawning of the so-called "Golden Age" of children's literature came, however, with the writings of Charles Kingsley, Lewis Carroll and George MacDonald (275). But fantasy, however, was not solely the literary province of children. Interestingly, both Kingsley and MacDonald also wrote novels for adults; Kingsley's *Alton Locke* contains some mythic dream sequences, while MacDonald's *Phantastes* and *Lilith* are both dream fantasies. These books "appealed to a society in which religious beliefs were being eroded and which had become disillusioned with the results of utilitarianism," Schenkel notes.[1] In an age where traditional beliefs and values were held up to question, and certainties were constantly undermined, Fantasy provided a way to "escape inwards," into the realms of the mind and the spirit.

Nineteenth century fantasy, in the tradition of which much twentieth century fantasy follows, arose out of a co-mingling of a number of "currents and eddies of thought" as Stephen Prickett demonstrates; from the Gothic tradition and Romanticism came the revival of mysticism and "a renewed feeling for the numinous—the irrational and mysterious elements in religious experience" (Prickett 10), and a revulsion (such as that so cogently and compellingly expressed in Blake's "Song of Experience"), towards the worst aspects of human exploitation and degradation which characterised the early Industrial Revolution. The tension between "Imagination" and "fantasy" which pervades Romanticism was sustained during the Victorian era, and the fantasists of that age turned the tension inward, inviting their readers to participate in worlds of wonder, of dreams and shadows. That Victorians were able to come to terms with the ambivalence between these two concepts, especially as they were played out in their art, literature and religion, was, as Prickett observes, "the greatest self-critical act of the age" (11).

The boundary between "Victorian" and "Twentieth Century" fantasy is somewhat blurred; Stephen Prickett includes in his list of "Victorian" fantasists the children's novelist Edith Nesbit, whose fantasies were written well into this century. In a collection of essays on the Victorian fantasists, which I have edited,[2] I have done the same. Colin Manlove, however, in his significant critical work *Modern Fantasy*, begins in the Victorian age, with Charles Kingsley; while David Pringle, in his broad overview of contemporary fantasy with the same title—*Modern Fantasy*—begins with Tolkien, in 1950.

It is not wholly surprising that this should be so, since many of the social, psychological and religious concerns of the previous century have become those of this century also. The dissolution of traditional beliefs, the sense of anxiety about the future, the realisation that science does not offer unproblematic "progress," and the high level of *angst* about the possibility of the destruction of the world either by nuclear war or by environmental vandalism that so permeates twentieth century consciousness, have all been inherited from the nineteenth century. H.G. Wells's invading, world-destroying Martians, living metaphors for destructive humanity, translated with little difficulty from nineteenth century Woking to twentieth century America, and his perennially popular novellette, *The Time Machine* also warned that the future was likely to be almost anything but bright, optimistic and hopeful.

The twentieth century has intensified the feelings of anxiety by giving humanity access to bigger and better means of self-destruction, and by providing more cogent and applicable scientific theories to debunk religion and to assert their own claims to dogmatic pre-eminence—claims which, in some countries, have contributed to the proscription of certain religious practices—such as the recitation of prayers in public (state-run) schools in the United States and also in Australia.

There have been other elements contributing to the decline in religious observance—among them, perhaps, the intrusion into human lives of the ubiquitous television set. Television stifles the Imagination, it is said, because it concentrates the attention of viewers on the external, and numbs the ability to heed the messages from the inner world of the intellect, the imagination and the spirit by limiting human experiences to what can be seen through the narrowed focus of the camera lens. As Ted Hughes puts it,

> . . . we sit, closely cramped in the cockpit behind the eyes, steering through the brilliantly crowded landscape beyond the [camera] lenses, focussed on details and distinctions. In the end, since all our attention from birth has been narrowed into that outward beam, we come to regard our body as no more than a somewhat stupid vehicle. All the urgent information coming towards us from that inner world sounds to us like a blank, or at best an occasional grunt, or a twinge. Because we have no equipment to receive it and decode it. The body, with its spirit, is the antennae of all perceptions, the receiving aerial for all wavelengths. But we are disconnected. (87)

What twentieth-century, television-educated humanity needs, Hughes suggests, is a faculty for recovering the magic of the inner world and harmonising it with our experiences of the outer world; keeping faith, as Hughes reminds us, quoting Goethe, "with the world of things and the world of spirits equally" (92). And we might achieve this by myth, legend and fantasy.

There is a school of thought which debunks myth and legend as mere lies. C.S. Lewis thought so: "lies breathed through silver," he called them before Tolkien taught him otherwise (Tolkien 49). The newspapermen and the historians think so, too. But the fantasists know that myth and legend are possibly the truest part of our inner selves. After all, literature is made up of imaginative constructs; even histories and biographies are written, however meticulously they may cite sources, from somebody's point of view and are therefore biased towards a certain set of beliefs about a particular set of circumstances or a particular person. Fiction consists of lies, relying on the convention of a "suspension of disbelief" for its credibility, no matter how "realistic" it purports to be. For example, life is not lived in neat, self-encapsulated chapters. So there is an argument for classifying all literature as "fantasy" in some sense or other, and for asserting that there is no discrete category that is uniquely "fantastical."

Nevertheless, important distinctions occur between what is acknowledged as "realistic" fiction and that classified as Fantasy.

"Realistic" fiction—or that which David Lodge, following Roman Jakobson, calls "metonymic" (Lodge, *passim*)—focuses the "lens" of human experience outwards in ways similar to that by which the television camera operates. It is, like metonymy, "the substitution of the part for the whole," contiguous with the outer experience of what we call "the real." Fantasy is, again to use the terms appropriated from Jakobson by Lodge, "metaphorical"—more like poetry than prose, as the influences on it by the Romantics might suggest. It sets up systems by which the Imagination is activated—not merely by the writer of fantastical stories but also by the reader who enters in to them and engages with the fantastical world. In fantasy, metaphors abound—metaphors by which the reader can confront the inner Self and actually experience (and not merely witness an experience of) the world of the wonderful and the marvellous. That, certainly, is the message of Ende's *The Neverending Story*, and his Fantastica certainly includes all fantastical worlds. It might even be said that in Ende's story, all theories of the Imagination and of Fantasy are actualised. In reading Fantasy, we all become types of an archetypal Bastian, able to bring back from the fantastical world the water of life.

This is, of course, the way Tolkien also sees Fantasy; this is his theory of "Recovery" brought to life in a fantasy text. The "Water of Life"—the rebirth, as it were, of the Imagination, refreshes and revives the mundane world in which we must pursue the business of living. But perhaps Tolkien's term "Escape" becomes problematical in this context. For the "escape" offered by Fantasy is not an escape out of but an escape into our spiritual selves. The journeys made available in Fantasy literature are inner journeys, into the hidden reaches of the human mind, into the far places of the human spirit. In each case readers are drawn into realms which are both compellingly beautiful and trepid with awe and horror, for such are the inner regions of human consciousness. If we make monsters, Barbara Johnson observes, we make them out of our own monstrosities (Johnson 151-154); we make Frankensteins out of terrors within us that cannot be otherwise expressed. And in Fantasy we can face and conquer our own monstrous self.

But in Fantasy, too, we discover what is good and beautiful within ourselves; like Orual in Lewis's *Till We Have Faces*, we look at our own glorious reflection in the crystal pool and know that "we also are Psyche," *the* psyche, what Socrates called "the true soul" (Guthrie 191-278). Fantasy is both confrontational and restorative, it is both disconcerting and healing. It leads us inwards so that we can function better outwardly. It is not surprising to find, as we do in so much late Victorian Fantasy, imagery that anticipates the psychologies of Freud and Jung (Prickett 11, Filmer 124 ff). And in this century, it is equally apparent that the same imagery is used in the most enduring fantasies—with Gollum as the Shadow of Frodo in *The Lord of the Rings*, and Orual as the Shadow of Psyche, in *Till We Have Faces*, and Ged and his Shadow in *The Earthsea Trilogy*.

What is also very clear about twentieth century Fantasy is the close correlation of myth, psychology and religion in the construction of human experiences. The three streams blend and merge at an undefinable point in a syncretism made possible by the working of the Imagination, blending, diffusing, recombining, creating. But in a world where it is difficult to formulate faith, impossible to apply dogmas, and painful to confront the self with self-knowledge, Fantasy takes over the task and makes the stories by which readers can tolerate self-knowledge, and through which they can be—if not made whole, then surely made aware of the ways by which they can heal themselves.

It may be that the solution is offered in terms redolent of pagan mysteries—the Great Mother, Nature, the Chymical Wedding; it may be that it is expressed through myths dating from the merging of paganism with Christianity, through the Holy Grail, or through the messianic wizard; it may be that modern myths "baptize" all older myths, as attempted by C.S. Lewis in his *Narnian Chronicles*, or in his spiritual worlds of celestial space. The power of "story" in Fantasy is, however, far greater than the theological origins from which it springs. As James B. Wiggins argues in his essay "Within and Without Stories,"

Stories present us with gifts. We may choose to manipulate them by skillfull interpretative devices, but stories that matter are greater than and outlive their interpretations. The temptation of theology has been to interpret the foundational stories given by religion and then to treat the interpretation as if it were that which was originally given. Perhaps that is what we have grown so tired of in theology and perhaps that is one of the contributing reasons for the return to stories in some quarters of the study of religion. (19)

Stories, we may conclude, are in and of themselves profoundly theological. As shown in this study, even in very sceptical texts, there is a theological point, and articulation of what is a profound theological virtue, hope. Hope is often written off as some kind of watery, anaemic virtue, somehow less than faith and weaker than love. And yet in the Christian scriptures, the three are mentioned in such a way as to suggest that they are interdependent, and that without hope, both faith and love are incomplete. But hope so elevated in this way is anything but weak, watery and anaemic. It is a scintillating virtue, the basis for enduring human relationships. After all, as St. Paul makes clear, "love hopes all things"; without hope, love would not be possible.

Stories, too, "judge" human activities by a peculiar moral code. Fantasy and fairy tale had a profound effect upon G.K. Chesterton, who wrote:

The things I believed most [in the nursery], the things I believe most now, are the things called fairy tales. They seem to me to be the entirely reasonable things. They are not fantasies [Chesterton uses the word in its pre-Victorian, pejorative sense, meaning delusions]: compared with them religion and rationalism are both abnormal, though religion is abnormally right and rationalism is abnormally wrong. Fairyland is nothing but the sunny country of common sense. It is not earth that judges heaven, but heaven that judges earth; so for me at least it was not earth that criticised elfland, but elfland that criticised the earth. (Chesterton 85)

Fantasy—in the sense which links it with the Imagination and with the world of Faerie—which is established according to what Chesterton calls "the ethics of Elfland" is not the material of mere entertainment, but rather the means by which we can focus upon the inner self and restore the balance between the human spirit and existence in the mundane world. In this anticipation of healing, of individuation, of wholeness, there is hope; as each text focuses upon ways to leave readers with some sense of resolution, even in such open-ended texts as *The Ancient Solitary Reign, The Mists of Avalon, The Last Unicorn, The Chymical Wedding,* and even, to some extent, *The Lord of the Rings* itself, there is some kind of hope offered, whether it be merely the hope for a better world, or for a better existence somewhere beyond the world. And in hope, as in the psychological and spiritual individuation that these texts also offer, there is healing.

One of the most important issues addressed in fantasy is that of language. Orwell, Lewis, Tolkien, Le Guin, Hoban and to some extent also Beagle, Vonnegut and L'Engle, draw attention to the way in which "our speech betrays us." Words are the building blocks by which the Imagination makes its marvellous worlds of fiction, and their importance is often overlooked, especially in this post-structuralist theoretical age when the notion of meaning is highly problematical; Fantasy, however, reminds us that the corruption of language signifies the corruption of the human spirit. But it reminds us, too, that words can also heal. They have an intrinsic power; whether that power is used for good or ill depends very much upon the choices made by those who speak them.

Tolkien understood the power of words; they are spells of great potency as he reminds us in his essay "On Fairy Stories." He also understood the power and importance of Fantasy in this century. Although his essay has obviously been written by a man filled with the enthusiasm of the religious convert, he gets it right on almost every count. He tends, perhaps, with his definition of Fantasy as *"pre-evangelium,"* to over-confidence in the consolations of religion. His definition of escape is not without problems; there are surely times when a prisoner is better imprisoned than set free. But if "Escape" is not seen so much as an escape from, but into, the deep places of the human mind and spirit, Tolkien is in accord with the writers who have followed him, and who have been influenced less by his essay than by his works of Fantasy. But I believe that he is right about the concept of "Recovery." Fantasy helps to balance the inner and the outer worlds, the inner and the outer experiences of its readers. And he is right in demonstrating how Fantasy is an activity of the creative Imagination, the Imagination as Coleridge conceived it, the "sub-creative," quasi-Divine faculty, "the refracted Light/ through [which] is splintered from a single White/ to many hues, and endlessly combines..." (49).

And Tolkien is right when he calls the process of sub-creation "Enchantment," producing "a Secondary World into which both designer and spectator can enter..." (48). Fantasy, however, does not seek to dominate or to control, but to open up, to share, to create for the pleasure of writer and reader alike:

> Of this desire the elves, in their better (but still perilous) part, are largely made; and it is from them that we may learn what is the central desire and aspiration of human Fantasy—even if the elves are, all the more in so far as they are, only a product of Fantasy itself. That creative desire is only cheated by counterfeits, whether the innocent but clumsy devices of the human dramatist, or the malevolent frauds of the magicians. In this world it is for men unsatisfiable, and so imperishable. Uncorrupted it does not seek delusion, not bewitchment and domination; it seeks shared enrichment, partners in making and delight...(49).

And so we create elves and hobbits and other kinds of "little people" to rehabilitate the child in ourselves, and with it something of the freshness of innocence and the transforming spiritual power of the Imagination. And most of all, true to the Romantic vision, the writers of Fantasy retain the robes of prophets and of priests, calling readers to self-knowledge, to transcendence and individuation, to a renewing of lost innocence, to hope for a better world.

The fantasies discussed in this book, then, have clearly appropriated the discourse of religion, its forms and its functions, to rehabilitate the visionary Imagination, the feeling intellect, the compassionate heart within its readers. Fantasy calls like Jonah to Nineveh for us to care for our world, for ourselves and each other, to enrich our understanding of all that it means to be human. Fantasy takes us into the mysteries of our own minds and spirits, and offers us individuation and healing. It makes the mundane world marvellous and takes from our eyes the veil of scepticism which has prevented us from believing that there are unicorns in our gardens. Some things, after all, have to be believed in order to be seen.

Twentieth-century Fantasy, then, is in a very real sense the voice of the age. It speaks the doubts and fears and conflicts which are part of the postmodern condition. In turn, however, it subverts the scepticism of the age by refusing to despair, and if religion has become hoarse from trying to be heard in a dissident crowd, Fantasy has appropriated its voice also. For Fantasy consistently articulates hope. It focuses on the inner world of the intellect, the Imagination and the Spirit, and it reminds us that no matter how bleak the circumstances might be, human beings can still create elves and gods and unicorns.

And while there is such magic abroad in the world, there is always the possibility that we might catch a glimpse of the marvellous unseen realm to which Fantasy takes us, and which Fantasy makes real. On the threshold of the Imagination, there is hope, for as Edith Nesbit reminds us in the epigraph to this chapter, that is the place where "anything may happen."

Notes

Chapter One

[1]Dr. Julian Bulnois had a phone-in radio program, "On the Other Side of the Couch," on Brisbane ABC station 4QR during 1986-87, in which these views were expressed.

[2]A new book by Kevin Hart, *The Trespass of the Sign* (Cambridge UP, 1989) discusses the relevance of contemporary literary theories to a negative theology. I do not believe, however, that the scepticism expressed in much contemporary fantasy literature addresses this concern; rather I believe it evinces affirmative metaphysics, the doubts raised pertaining rather to the beneficent nature of God or the gods in relation to human experience and hope.

[3]See David Jasper, "Making Words Mean a Great Deal" a Preface to *The Victorian Fantasists*, Kath Filmer, ed., (London: MacMillan, 1991).

Chapter Two

[1]Although Stephen Prickett has argued in his *Words and the Word* (Cambridge UP, 1986) that the roles of priest and prophet were one and the same, there is other evidence to suggest that they were not. For example, B.W. Anderson notes, "A priest could officiate at sacred rites, teach the people the traditions of the past, and manipulate the sacred lot in answer to yes or no questions. But the prophet, speaking under the influence of Yarweh's spirit, was able to interpret the meaning of events and to proclaim the will of God in concrete terms" (*The Living World of the Old Testament*, 3rd Ed., London: Longman, 1984, 231). There were occasions when priests prophesied; but essentially the priest was a priest by virtue of heredity, the line of Zadok, appointed by Solomon, while the prophets were called by God (See Amos 1: 3-5; Jeremiah 2: 1-2; Isaiah 45: 11-13).

Chapter Three

[1]See Kath Filmer, *The Polemic Image: The Role of Metaphor and Symbol in the Rhetoric of the Fiction of C.S. Lewis.* Unpublished Ph.D. thesis. The University of Queensland, 1985.

[2]The classical island which is known in Classical literature as The Fortunate Isles or the Isles of the Blest is the happy dwelling place of the thrice-born who have each time attained Elysium; see Robert Graves, *Greek Myths: Illustrated Edition* (London: Cassell, 1984), 41. The Irish legendary island of Hy-Brasil closely parallels the classical image. It was the island which the Garden of Eden became after the Fall of Adam and Eve, set in the West; see Henry Kendall, "Hy-Brasil" in *Selections from the Australian Poets*, Bertram Stevens and George MacKaness, eds., (Sydney: Angus and Robertson, c. 1940), 149-50. Kendall's note on Hy-Brasil is included in the appendix, 193.

[3]See "An Allegory Unveiled: A Reading of J.R.R. Tolkien's *The Lord of the Rings*," in *The Ring Bearer: Journal of The Inner Ring—The Mythopoeic Literature Society of Australia*, 3: 3, Spring 1985, 2-8, in which I argue that the Elves in some ways symbolise in function the activities of the Church, especially in the Catholic tradition. The lembas, or waybread, and the miruvor, or healing drink, can be seen as representations or

anticipations of the sacrament of the Eucharist which provides spiritual sustenance. The gist of my argument in this paper is, of course, that the quest of *The Lord of the Rings* is a spiritual quest—the quest to rid humanity individually and at large of the "Ring" of Original Sin.

[4]In 1983, some ephemeral newsletters published in Brisbane, Australia, under the title of "The Christian Fundamentalist," denounced both C.S. Lewis and J.R.R. Tolkien as witches because of their use of "magic" in their books—magic being seen as the work of evil and not a symbol (as the authors intended) for the supernatural and the power of God.

Chapter Four

[1]There are several right wing "think tanks" bearing Lewis's name. This information was given to me by the Rt. Rev. Alastair Haggart, former Archbishop of Scotland, in a conversation on November 5, 1988. Bishop Haggart had been a recipient of material from one of these groups, and material he showed me was clearly fundamentalist in religious orientation and right wing in its political views.

[2]Douglas Gresham's views have been made public through addresses made under the sponsorship of the Marion E. Wade Center at Wheaton College, Illinois. The Center houses a vast collection of materials associated with seven British Christian authors—Lewis, Tolkien, Williams, Dorothy L. Sayers, George MacDonald, Chesterton and Eliot.

[3]"To Owen Barfield," unpubl. letter dated May 29, 1928. In the Bodleian Library, MS FACS 53, 95.

[4]For example, goddess and/or "earth mother" characters include Mrs. Dimble and Grace Ironwood in *That Hideous Strength*, Sarah Smith of Golders Green in *The Great Divorce* and The Green Lady (Tinidril) in *Perelandra*. Sexually predatory females are more common: the Brown girls in *The Pilgrim's Regress*, the lesbian Fairy Hardcastle in *That Hideous Strength*, Susan Pevensie in the Narnian Chronicles (at least by association with worldly values), Peggy in the short story "The Shoddy Lands," and the Thin Woman and the Fat Woman in "Ministering Angels."

[5]One of the most important studies to emerge in recent years is Peter J. Schakel's *Reason and Imagination in C.S. Lewis: A Study of Till We Have Faces* (Grand Rapids: Eerdmans, 1984), although chapters on the novel appear in most other works dealing with Lewis's fictional *oeuvre*.

[6]I have discussed this point in more detail in "A Prophet for the Postmodern: Scepticism and Belief in Charles Williams's *The Place of the Lion*," to appear in *Essays on Charles Williams*, Peter J. Schakel and Charles Huttar, eds., (Hope College, Holland, Michigan).

Chapter Six

[1]Stephen Prickett, in a keynote address to the Fifth Annual International Conference of The Inner Ring: The Mythopoeic Literature Society of Australia, King's College, The University of Queensland, May 14-16, 1989. His topic, and the theme of the Conference, was "The Spirit of Place in Mythopoeic Literature."

[2]Tolkien argues that drama is not the best vehicle for Fantasy, and applies this comment to a production of *Puss in Boots* in which the transformations were patently obvious ("On Fairy Stories" 46).

[3]As well as his article in *Extrapolation*, Lake has also reviewed Hoban's book for *Foundation* 29, November 1983: 96-98, making many of the same points.

Chapter Seven

[1]This chapter is largely based upon my paper "That Hideous 1984: The Influence of C.S. Lewis's *That Hideous Strength* on George Orwell's *Nineteen Eighty-Four*" in *Extrapolation* 26: 2 (Summer, 1985): 160-169.

Chapter Nine

[1]See Wayne C. Booth. *A Rhetoric of Irony*. (Chicago: U of Chicago P, 1974), 61-63.

[2]See Raymond N. Olderman, "Out of the Waste Land. Peter S. Beagle, *The Last Unicorn*" in *Beyond the Waste Land: A Study of the American Novel in the Nineteen Sixties* (New Haven: Yale UP, 1972), 220-242.

[3]See Florence McCullough, *Medieval Latin and French Bestiaries* (Chapel Hill: U of North Carolina P, 1962): "All Versions [of medieval Bestiaries] agree that Christ is the Spiritual Unicorn..." (179).

Chapter Ten

[1]The paper "George Orwell" was originally published in *Time and Tide*, January 8, 1955, in response to a televised version of *Nineteen Eighty-Four*. Lewis writes that he much preferred *Animal Farm* because of its mythic qualities. The article is reprinted in *Of This and Other Worlds*, Walter Hooper, ed., (London: Collins, 1982), 133-37.

[2]Note the subtitle of Orwell's work: *Animal Farm: A Fairy Story*. Fp 1945. (Harmondsworth: Penguin, 1941).

[3]In the 1950s, Lewis was regarded as a "Conservative" for his opposition to environmental destruction, experimentation on animals, and the misuse of science. of science.

Chapter Eleven

[1]See Kathleen Raine, *Blake and the New Age* (London: George Allen and Unwin, 1979).

[2]See, for example, Valery Medvedev, *Barankin's Fantasy World: Two Stories*. Trans. Kathleen Cook (USSR: Raduga, 1986).

Chapter Twelve

[1]Schenkel is here following the argument developed by Humphrey Carpenter in his study of *Secret Gardens: The Golden Age of Children's Literature* (London: Allen and Unwin, 1985).

[2]See *The Victorian Fantasists: Essays on Culture, Society and Belief in the Mythopoeic Literature of the Victorian Age*, Kath Filmer, ed., (London: Macmillan, 1991).

Works Cited

Chapter One

Coleridge, Samuel Taylor. *Biographia Literaria*. Edited with his Aesthetical Essays by J. Shawcross, in two volumes. London: Oxford UP, 1907, 1967, Vol. 1.

Ellis, John M. "What Does Deconstruction Contribute to Theory of Criticism?" *New Literary History* 19: 2 (Winter 1988).

Frankl, Viktor. *Man's Search for Meaning*. Trans. Ilse Lasch. London: Hodder and Stoughton, 1946, 1959, 1962.

Handelman, Susan A. *The Slayers of Moses: The Emergence of Rabbinic Interpretation in Modern Literary Theory*. Albany: State U of New York P, 1982.

Miller, J. Hillis. "The Poetry of Reality." *Literature and Religion*. Ed. Giles B. Gunn. New York: Harper and Row, 1971. 191-210.

Jasper, David. *Coleridge as a Poet and Religious Thinker: Inspiration and Revelation*. Basingstoke: MacMillan, 1985.

MacDonald, George. *Lilith: A Romance*. 1895. Grand Rapids: Eerdmans, 1981.

Scott, Nathan A., Jr. "Poetry and Prayer." *Literature and Religion*. Ed. Giles B. Gunn. New York: Harper and Row, 1971. 177-190.

Chapter Two

Barthes, Roland. "The Death of the Author?" 1969. *Modern Criticism and Theory: A Reader*. Ed. David Lodge. London: Longman, 1988. 167-172.

Carpenter, Humphrey. *The Inklings: C.S. Lewis, J.R.R. Tolkien, Charles Williams, and their Friends*. London: Allen and Unwin, 1978.

Coleridge, S.T. *Selected Poetry and Prose of Coleridge*. Edited with an Introduction, by Donald A. Staeffer. New York: Random House, 1951.

Eco, Umberto. *Foucault's Pendulum*. Trans. William Weaver. London: Secker and Warburg, 1989.

Foucault, Michel. "What is an Author?" 1969. *Modern Criticism and Theory: A Reader*. Ed. David Lodge. London: Longman, 1988. 197-210.

Harris, Wilson. *The Womb of Space: The Cross-Cultural Imagination*. Contributions in Afro-American Studies No. 73. Westport, CT.: Greenwood, 1983.

Le Guin, Ursula. "Why are Americans Afraid of Dragons?" *The Language of the Night: Essays on Fantasy and Science Fiction*. Ed. Susan Wood. New York: Perigree, 1979.

Lewis, C.S. *An Experiment in Criticism*. Cambridge: Cambridge UP, 1961.

_____ *Miracles: A Preliminary Study*. Glasgow: Collins Fount, 1960.

_____ "On Stories." *Of This and Other Worlds*. Ed. Walter Hooper. London: Collins, 1982.

Prickett, Stephen. *Coleridge and Wordsworth: The Poetry of Growth*. Cambridge: Cambridge UP, 1970.

Norris, Christopher. *Deconstruction: Theory and Practice*. London: Methuen, 1982.

Scholes, Robert. *Textual Power: Literary Theory and the Teaching of English*. New Haven: Yale UP, 1985.

Shelley, Percy Bysshe."A Defense of Poetry." *The Selected Poetry and Prose of Shelley*. Ed. with an Introduction, by Harold Bloom. New York: New American Library, 1966.

Tolkien, J.R.R. "On Fairy Stories." *Tree and Leaf*. London: Allen and Unwin, 1964.

Wordsworth, William. *Selected Poems and Prefaces*. Edited with an Introduction and Notes, by Jack Stillinger. Boston: Houghton Mifflin, 1965.

Chapter Three

Carpenter, Humphrey. *The Inklings: C.S. Lewis, J.R.R. Tolkien, Charles Williams, and their Friends*. London: George Allen and Unwin, 1978.

———— *J.R.R. Tolkien: A Biography*. London: George Allen and Unwin, 1980.

Filmer, Kath. "An Allegory Unveiled: J.R.R. Tolkien's *The Lord of the Rings*." *The Ring Bearer: Journal of The Inner Ring—The Mythopoeic Literature Society of Australia* 3:3. (Spring 1985): 2-5.

———— *The Polemic Image: The Role of Metaphor and Symbol in the Rhetoric of the Fiction of C.S. Lewis*. Unpublished Ph.D. thesis, The University of Queensland, 1985.

Lake, David. "Coincidence, Hairsbreadth, Cliffhanger: Tolkien's Narrative Style." *The Ring Bearer: Journal of The Inner Ring—The Mythopoeic Literature Society of Australia* 6:3 (Spring 1988): 20-25.

Strugnell, John. "The Forms of Evil." In *The Ring Bearer: Journal of The Inner Ring—The Mythopoeic Literature Society of Australia* 1:3 (Spring 1983): 15.

Tolkien, J.R.R. *The Lord of the Rings*. (One volume ed.) 1954, 1955. London: George Allen and Unwin, 1981.

———— "On Fairy Stories." *Tree and Leaf*. London: George Allen and Unwin, 1964.

Chapter Four

Carpenter, Humphrey. *The Inklings: C.S. Lewis, J.R.R. Tolkien, Charles Williams and their Friends*. London: George Allen and Unwin, 1978.

Derrida, Jacques."Structure, Sign and Play in the Discourse of the Human Sciences." *The Structuralist Controversy: The Language of Criticism and the Sciences of Man*. Eds. Richard Macksey and Eugenio Donato. Baltimore: Johns Hopkins UP, 1972.

Douglas, J.D. *et al*, eds. *The New International Dictionary of the Christian Church*. Grand Rapids: Zondervan, 1978.

Filmer, Kath. *The Polemic Image: The Role of Metaphor and Symbol in the Rhetoric of the Fiction of C.S. Lewis*. Unpublished Ph.D. thesis, The University of Queensland, 1985.

Hannay, Margaret. " 'Surprised by Joy': C.S. Lewis's Changing Attitude Toward Women." *Mythlore* 4: 1 (1976): 15-20.

Heath-Stubbs, John. *Charles Williams*. Writers and Their Work, No. 63. London: Longmans, 1955.

Lewis, C.S. *God in the Dock: Essays on Theology and Ethics*. Ed. Walter Hooper. Grand Rapids: Eerdmans, 1970.

———— *Letters of C.S. Lewis*. Ed. W.H. Lewis. London: Bles, 1966.

———— *The Pilgrim's Regress: An Allegorical Apology for Christianity, Reason and Romanticism*. 1933, 1943. Grand Rapids: Eerdmans, 1981.

———— *Poems*. Ed. Walter Hooper. New York: Harcourt Brace Jovanovich, 1964.

_____ *Till We Have Faces: A Myth Retold.* London: Bles, 1956.

MacDonald, George. *Lilith: A Romance.* 1895. Grand Rapids: Eerdmans, 1981.

_____ *Phantastes: A Faerie Romance for Men and Women.* 1858. Grand Rapids: Eerdmans, 1981.

_____ *The Princess and Curdie.* London: Collins, 1958.

Schakel, Peter J. *Reason and Imagination in C.S. Lewis: A Study of* Till We Have Faces. Grand Rapids: Eerdmans, 1984.

Tolkien, J.R.R. *The Lord of the Rings.* (One volume ed.) 1954, 1955. London: George Allen and Unwin, 1980.

Williams, Charles. *He Came Down From Heaven.* London: Heinemann, 1938.

_____ *The Place of the Lion.* 1933. New York: Pelligrini, 1951.

Chapter Five

Blake, William. "The Marriage of Heaven and Hell." *The Complete Poetry and Prose of William Blake.* Ed. David V. Erdman. (Newly Revised Ed.) Berkeley and Los Angeles: U of California P, 1982.

Coleridge, Samuel Taylor. "The Ancient Mariner." *Lyrical Ballads.* The text of the 1798 ed., with Introduction, Notes and Appendices, by R.L. Brett and A.R. Jones. London: Methuen, 1965. 9-35.

Gaskell, G.A. *Dictionary of All Scriptures and Myths.* New York: Avenel, 1981.

Hoff, Benjamin. *The Tao of Pooh.* London: Methuen, 1984.

Le Guin, Ursula. *The Earthsea Trilogy: A Wizard of Earthsea* (1968), *The Tombs of Atuan* (1972), *The Farthest Shore* (1973). Harmondsworth: Penguin, 1979.

_____ *The Language of the Night.* Ed. Susan Wood. New York: Putnam's, 1979.

Lewis, C.S. *The Last Battle.* 1956. New York: Collier, 1970.

_____ *Prince Caspian.* London: Collins, 1961.

Lowentrout, Peter M. "The Influence of Speculative Fiction on the Religious Formation of the Young: A Preliminary Statistical Investigation." *Extrapolation* 28:4 (1987): 345-359.

Prickett, Stephen. *Coleridge and Wordsworth: The Poetry of Growth.* Cambridge: Cambridge UP, 1970.

Chapter Six

Lord Acton. *Historical Essays and Studies.* London: MacMillan, 1908.

Carroll, Lewis. *The Annotated Alice: Alice's Adventures in Wonderland* and *Through the Looking Glass.* Ed. with Intro. and Notes, by Martin Gardner. Harmondsworth: Penguin, 1970.

Filmer, Kath. "From Belbury to Bernt Arse: the Rhetoric of the Wasteland in Lewis, Orwell and Hoban." *Mythlore* 52. 14:2 (Winter, 1987): 19-26.

Hoban, Russell. *The Mouse and His Child.* Harmondsworth: Puffin, 1976.

_____ *Riddley Walker.* London: Picador, 1982.

Lake, David. "Making the Two One: Language and Mysticism in *Riddley Walter.*" *Extrapolation* 25:2 (1984): 157-170.

_____ "Review: *Riddley Walker* and *Pilgermann* by Russell Hoban." *Foundation* 29. Nov. 1983: 96-98.

Morrissey, Thomas J. "Armageddon from Huxley to Hoban." *Extrapolation* 25:3 (1984): 197-213.

Prickett, Stephen. "The Inversion of Worlds Empirical Philosophy Through the Looking Glass in *The Enchanted Wood: the Value and Appeal of Mythopoeic Literature.*" Proceedings of "The Enchanted Wood" Conference of The Inner

Ring: The Mythopoeic Literature Society of Australia. Ed. Kath Filmer. English Dept. U of Queensland 1985. 88-99.

Chapter Seven

Bowles, Colin. "Newspeak." *The Australian Magazine*. April 7-8, 1990: 43-46.

Charlton, Peter. "From War, a Memory of Courage and Mates." *Anzac* Supplement to *The Courier-Mail*, Brisbane. 25 April 1990: 17-18.

Chilton, Paul. *Orwellian Language and the Media*. London: Pluto, 1988.

Druker, Barry. "The Oaken Bucket and the Crystal Spirit: The Political Art of G.K. Chesterton and George Orwell." *The Chesterton Review* 10, August 1984. 24-64.

Filmer, Kath. "From Belbury to Bernt Arse: the Rhetoric of the Wasteland in Lewis, Orwell and Hoban." *Mythlore* 52. 14:2 (Winter, 1987): 19-26.

——— "That Hideous 1984: The Influence of C.S. Lewis's *That Hideous Strength* on George Orwell's *Nineteen Eighty-Four.*" *Extrapolation* 26:2 (Summer, 1985): 160-169.

Gilfedder, John. "Encounters with the Mind of C.S. Lewis." *The Ring Bearer: Journal of the Mythopoeic Literature Society of Australia* 1:3 (Spring, 1983).

Green, Roger Lancelyn and Walter Hooper. *C.S. Lewis: A Biography*. Glasgow: Fount, 1979.

Golding, Peter and Philip Elliott. *Making the News*. London: Longman, 1979.

Huxley, Aldous. *Letters of Aldous Huxley*. Ed. Grover Smith. London: Chatto and Windus, 1969.

Lewis, C.S. *The Abolition of Man: or Reflections on Education with special reference to the teaching of English in the Upper Forms of Schools*. 1943. Glasgow: Fount, 1978.

——— *That Hideous Strength: A Modern Fairy Story for Grown Ups*. London: The Bodley Head, 1945.

Orwell, George. *Nineteen Eighty-Four: A Novel*. 1949. Harmondsworth: Penguin, 1954.

——— "Politics and the English Language." April 1946. *Inside the Whale and Other Essays*. Harmondsworth: Penguin, 1962. 143-158.

——— "Politics vs. Literature: An Examination of *Gulliver's Travels.*" September 1946. *Inside the Whale and Other Essays* Harmondsworth: Penguin, 1962. 121-142.

——— "The Scientist Takes Over" (Review of C.S. Lewis's *That Hideous Strength*). *The Manchester Evening News*, 16 August 1945: 2.

Stansky, Peter and William Abrahams. *Orwell: The Transformation*. London: Granada, 1981.

Chapter Eight

Baum, L. Frank. *The Wizard of Oz*. 1900. New York: Award Books, Undated.

Ende, Michael. *The Neverending Story*. 1979. Trans. Ralph Manheim. London: Allen Lane, 1983.

Filmer, Kath. "Beware the Nothing: An Allegorical Reading of Michael Ende's *The Neverending Story.*" *The Ring Bearer: Journal of the Mythopoeic Literature Society of Australia* 4:1. (March, 1986): 29-33.

Harari, Josue V. "Critical Factions/Critical Fictions." *Textual Strategies: Perspectives in Post-Structuralist Criticism*. Ed. Hosue V. Harari. Ithaca, NY: Cornell UP, 1979.

Jasper, David. *Coleridge as Poet and Religious Thinker: Inspiration and Revelation.* London: MacMillan, 1985.

Lewis, C.S. *The Last Battle.* 1956. New York: Collier, 1976.

———. "Preface." *The Pilgrim's Regress: An Allegorical Apology for Christianity Reason and Romanticism,* 3rd ed. London: Bles, 1943.

Nuttall, A.D. *A New Mimesis: Shakespeare and the Representation of Reality.* London: Methuen, 1983.

Prickett, Stephen. *Coleridge and Wordsworth: The Poetry of Growth.* Cambridge UP, 1970.

Thorpe, Douglas. "Dorothy's Blakean Dream." *The Ring Bearer: Journal of the Mythopoeic Literature Society of Australia* 3:2 (June 1985) 13, 16.

Chapter Nine

Beagle, Peter. *The Last Unicorn.* London: Unwin, 1982.

Booth, Wayne C. *A Rhetoric of Irony.* Chicago: U of Chicago P, 1974.

Lodge, David. "A Kind of Business." *Review: Criticism in Society* Imre Salunsinzky. Interviews. London: Methuen, 1987. *Scripsi* 5:1 (March 1988): 109-120. (113).

McCullough, Florence. *Medieval Latin and French Bestiaries.* Chapel Hill: U of North Carolina P, 1962.

Klindowitz, Jerome. *Kurt Vonnegut.* London: Methuen 193?.

Olderman, Raymond M. *Beyond the Waste Land: A Study of the American Novel in the Nineteen Sixties.* New Haven: Yale UP, 1972.

Thurber, James. *The 13 Clocks and the Wonderful O.* 1951, 1958. London: Hamish Hamilton, 1945.

———. *The Thurber Carnival.* London: Hamish Hamilton, 1945.

Vonnegut, Kurt, Jr. *Cat's Cradle* 1963. Harmondsworth: Penguin, 1965.

Chapter Ten

Boston, Lucy. *The Children of Green Knowe.* 1958. Harmondsworth: Puffin, 1976.

———. *An Enemy at Green Knowe.* 1964. Harmondsworth: Puffin, 1977.

———. *The River at Green Knowe.* 1959. Harmondsworth: Puffin, 1976.

———. *The Stones of Green Knowe.* 1976. Harmondsworth: Penguin, 1979.

———. *A Stranger at Green Knowe.* 1961. Harmondsworth: Puffin, 1977.

Chesterton, G.K. *Orthodoxy.* London: John Lane the Bodley Head, 1909.

Cooper, Susan. *The Dark is Rising.* 1965. Harmondsworth: Puffin, 1976.

———. *Greenwitch.* 1974. Harmondsworth: Puffin, 1977.

———. *The Grey King.* 1975. Harmondsworth: Puffin, 1977.

———. *Over Sea, Under Stone.* 1965. Harmondsworth: Puffin, 1968.

———. *Silver on the Tree.* 1977. Harmondsworth: Puffin, 1979.

Garner, Alan. *Elidor.* 1965. London: Fontana Lions, 1974.

———. *The Owl Service.* 1967. London: Fontana Lions, 1973.

Kelly, Tony. *A New Imagining: Towards and Australian Spirituality.* Melbourne: Collins Dove, 1990.

L'Engle, Madeleine. *A Swiftly Tilting Planet.* 1978. New York: Laurel Leaf, 1979.

———. *A Wind in the Door.* 1973. New York: Laurel Leaf, 1976.

———. *A Wrinkle in Time.* 1962. Harmondsworth: Puffin, 1967.

Lewis, C.S. *The Discarded Image: An Introduction to Medieval and Renaissance Literature.* Cambridge: Cambridge UP, 1969.

———. *The Lion, the Witch and the Wardrobe.* 1950. London: Collins, 1965.

———. *The Narnian Chronicles* (seven volumes). New York: Collier, 1970.

_____ *Of This and Other Worlds*. Ed. Walter Hooper. London: Collins, 1982.

_____ *Spirits in Bondage*. (Under the *nom-de-plume* of Clive Hamilton). London: Heinemann, 1919.

Prior, Natalie. "The Eagle Forever: Myth and Place in the Novels of Alan Garner" *The Enchanted Wood: The Value and Appeal of Mythopoeic Literature*. Proceedings of the First Annual International Conference of The Inner Ring: The Mythopoeic Literature Society of Australia. Ed. Kath Filmer. St. Lucia: The Inner Ring, 1985. 16-24.

Propp, Vladimir. *Mythology of the Folk Tale*. First ed. trans. Laurence Scott, with Intro. by Scatava Pirkova-Tacobson; Second ed. revised and ed. with Preface by Louis A. Wagner, with new Intro. by Alan Dundas. Austin: U of Texas P, 1979.

Tolkien, J.R.R. *The Hobbit, or There and Back Again*. London: Unwin, 1975.

_____ "On Fairy Stories." *Tree and Leaf*. London: George Allen and Unwin, 1964. 11-72.

Wordsworth, William. "Intimations of Immortality from Recollections of Early Childhood" *Selected Poems and Prefaces*. Ed. Jack Stillinger. Boston: Houghton Mifflin, 1965.

Wrightson, Patricia. *A Little Fear*. 1983. Ringwood, Vic.: Puffin, 1985.

_____ *The Nargun and the Stars*. 1973. Ringwood: Puffin, 1975.

_____ *An Older Kind of Magic*. 1972. Ringwood: Puffin, 1974.

Chapter Eleven

Bennett, Laura Gilmour. *A Wheel of Stars*. London: Viking, 1989.

Bradley, Marion. *The Mists of Avalon*. London: Michael Joseph, 1982.

Churton, Tobias. *The Gnostics*. London: Weidenfeld and Nicholas, 1987.

Clarke, Lindsay. *The Chymical Wedding*. London: Jonathan Cape, 1989.

Hocke, Martin. *The Ancient Solitary Reign*. London: Grafton, 1989.

Robbins, Tom. *Skinny Legs and All*. New York: Bantam, 1990.

Chapter Twelve

Filmer, Kath. "*La Belle Dame Sans Merci*: Cultural Criticism and the Mythopoeic Imagination in George MacDonald's *Lilith*." *The Victorian Fantasists: Culture, Society and Belief in the Mythopoeic Literature of the Victorian Age*. Ed. Kath Filmer. London: MacMillan, 1991.

Guthrie, W.K.C. *Socrates and Plato: The John Macrossan Memorial Lecture, 1957*. Brisbane: U of Queensland P, 1958.

Hughes, Ted. "Myth and Education." *Writers, Critics and Children: Articles from Children's Literature in Education*. Eds. Geoff Fox, et al. New York: Agathon, 1979.

Johnson, Barbara. *A World of Difference*. Baltimore: Johns Hopkins UP, 1987.

Lodge, David. *The Modes of Modern Writing: Metaphor, Metonymy and the Typology of Literature*. London: Edward Arnold, 1977.

Manlove, C.N. *Modern Fantasy: Five Studies*. Cambridge: Cambridge UP, 1975.

Nesbit, E. *The Enchanted Castle*. 1907. London: Ernest Benn, 1956.

Prickett, Stephen. *Victorian Fantasy*. Hassocks, Sx.: Harvester, 1979.

Schenkel, Elmar. "Domesticating the Supernatural: Functions of Magic in Nesbit's Children's Books." *The Victorian Fantasists: Culture, Society and Belief in the Mythopoeic Literature of the Victorian Age*. Ed. Kath Filmer. London: MacMillan, 1991.

Tolkien, J.R.R. *Tree and Leaf.* London: George Allen and Unwin, 1964.

Wiggins, James B. "Within and Without Stories." *Religion as Story.* Ed. James B. Wiggins. New York: Harper and Row, 1975.

Index